Why Sammy Still Can't Read

A Service Delivery Model
for Creating a Culture of Reading

Leroy McClure, CALT, LDT,

and Yvette McClure, MBA

First published by Dog Ear Publishing
4011 Vincennes Road
Indianapolis, IN 46268
www.dogearpublishing.net

ISBN: 978-145756-683-7

This book is printed on acid-free paper.
Printed in the United States of America

This book is dedicated to
my brother, Sammy, or should I say, Sam.

Table of Contents

Dear Sam,

I had no idea.... I didn't understand why you struggled to read as we were growing up in Conway, Arkansas. Your undiagnosed dyslexia caused you to experience frustration, anxiety, tension, pain, and agony daily for many years. To this day, it's heartbreaking to me, and I find myself apologizing to you over and over.

Since we were only 13 months apart in age, I couldn't empathize with what you were going through. I knew something was different. I recognized that the reading and math skills that were so easy for me created frustration, anxiety, and tension for you. I witnessed your pain and agony and could not do anything about it. Again, I find myself apologizing to you over and over.

I realize that me being an A student didn't help you at all. It created a huge gap in our relationship as mom and dad used me as the standard when it came to learning. Because you were only one grade behind me, our parents, siblings, and even our teachers always compared you to me. It wasn't fair, nor was it right. While I was one of the smartest students in my class, you were at the bottom of yours. As you struggled learning how to read, complete your homework, do a task around the house, or remember things, you were always tormented by the unfair comparisons to me. I now know that wasn't easy for you.

Once again, I find myself repeatedly apologizing to you. I am sorry, Sam.

Yes, Sam, I remember being at our family gatherings where you shared stories with those who didn't know you well. As you recalled your experience, you told it with such excitement and compelling explanations for those who had no first-hand knowledge of the situation. During your conversations, all of us noticed that the facts of your stories didn't align with how the situation actually occurred. You either embellished or even deleted parts of your stories. It felt like you were sharing a different experience—one of which we had no knowledge. You viewed and heard things that we didn't see nor hear. While you weren't known as a liar, some people questioned your ability to tell the truth, because telling altered stories were a common occurrence with you. I was one of those people who didn't understand how your mind worked. Again, I find myself apologizing to you. I am sorry, Sam.

The more I reminisce, the more I find myself offering an apology. I now realize you possessed the characteristics of dyslexia, dyscalculia, attention-deficit hyperactive disorder (ADHD), and auditory processing disorder. You are a very bright young man, but the fact remains that you learn differently than others. Sam, like many other people, you grew up with an undiagnosed learning disability, struggling to read, being misunderstood and unfairly measured up to those who didn't struggle in those areas, and growing up in my shadow. It had to be truly a living nightmare for you. Because I now know about different learning styles and learning disabilities, I promise I'll help students like you receive the proper diagnosis early and create a successful academic intervention plan to help ensure that they'll learn to read, write, compute math, and be better prepared to enter college or the workforce.

Sam, I love you,

Leroy

Preface

If the truth is told, numerous people could write a letter very similar to the one that I wrote to my brother, Sam. I am now a man on a new mission—an urgent one. My mission is to help liberate thousands of people from experiencing the pain and agony that Sam experienced daily while growing up in Conway, Arkansas, as a struggling reader. Thanks to my brother Sam, I am waging a war to eradicate illiteracy one child at a time.

When we think about Sam and others who have a disability, we picture someone who is physically impaired. Merriam-Webster defines a disability as "a physical, mental, cognitive, or developmental condition that impairs, interferes with, or limits a person's ability to engage in certain tasks or actions or participate in typical daily activities and interactions." A disability substantially affects a person's life activities, and some disorders may be present from birth and/or manifest themselves anytime during a person's lifetime. Someone with a physical disability can be easily seen with the naked eye, and people instantly form an opinion based on what they see. This opinion might be that the person is unable to walk, talk, see, etc. When you recognize someone as having a physical disability, your mind formulates either a positive or negative judgment.

Learning Disabilities (LD) and Attention-Deficit/Hyperactive Disorder (ADHD) are so prevalent in our world today. A high percentage of time, you maybe interacting with someone with such a disorder, and you're not even aware of it. Unfortunately, someone who has LD or ADHD is hard to detect with the naked eye—it's harder to identify the signs and symptoms. However, usually, your speculation about this person's behavior can be directly related to his or her challenge. You can quickly judge them unfairly or even discriminate against them. Such a person is perceived as being "normal," thus you likely have the same expectations of this person as you would with anyone else. In the school system or the workplace, there's no simple way to tell if this person needs to be treated differently just from your mere or occasional observations.

Often, people with LD or ADHD are miseducated, mistreated, and misunderstood. These people are the epitome of Sammy. They are miseducated in the school system because teachers aren't adequately trained to recognize their learning challenges, and therefore, no remediation takes place. In the workplace, they are mistreated because of their subpar job performance due to their inability to comprehend or stay focused; therefore, they are likely overlooked for job promotions and/or even fired. Such people are misunderstood in our society because society tends to see their irrational behavior and pass judgment on them instead of seeking to understand that person. We tend to gloss over these people, leaving a trail of criticism and/or hurt feelings.

According to the National Institute of Child Health and Human Development, 15 to 20 percent of Americans have a learning disability and other learning disorders. (How many people are affected/at risk for learning disabilities? 2016) Thus, if the U.S. population is 300 million people, then 15 percent or 45 million people could have LD or ADHD. Meaning, 1 out of 6 people that you encounter daily could have a learning disorder. (2017 World Population Data Sheet 2017) In our world, this group of people is ostracized and usually left behind to further drown as underachievers. Some may even fall through the cracks and end up in our penal system. An LD or ADHD is not a dismal disorder.

Beginning, struggling, or on-grade-level readers need the practical skills to cope with the increasing demands of the local, state, and national testing to graduate from high school and matriculate into college or the working world. Schools are ineffective regarding offering simple, not to mention specialized, programs for nonreaders who aren't on their grade level due to an undiagnosed or diagnosed learning challenge, low socio-economic conditions, and/or behavior. Creating a culture of reading isn't easy. However, simple solutions do exist, requiring a willingness on the part of the teachers, administrators, and school governance to develop and implement intervention programs that provide teacher training, creatively adjust the school's schedule, and buy student materials, all with ample time and on a small budget.

Using my knowledge and 30-plus years of experience, along with my team of experts at Triple A Educational Services, Inc. (TAES), I've adopted guidelines to implement a service delivery model for reading during or after school. TAES serves as an advocacy group and has developed best-practices implementation models of reading to support schools as well as any organization's after-school program. The goal of TAES's service delivery model is to provide support programs at every school and enable parents to live in a community with a school of their choice that embraces and values all students. TAES believes it begins with students learning a research-based reading program that enables them to thrive as good readers.

My primary objective is to shed light on how people who learn differently and those who live or work with them can turn this adversity into victory and problems into opportunities, thus creating winners even in losing situations.

In this book, I'm going to guide teachers and administrators through the practical steps to help struggling or challenged students at any school or organization. My proven service models can be efficiently and effectively integrated within a whole school or a small group. In reading this book, you'll come away with specific strategy-driven techniques for a small, medium, or large public, private, or charter school that you can use to implement a service model without placing a strenuous burden on your staff or budget. My goal is for teachers, administrators, and parents to become re-energized and prepared to advance their school or organization by transforming it into a culture of reading. In creating this culture of reading, educators can restore a learning disabled student's confidence in reading and ultimately improve local, state, and national test results for all students.

Why Sammy Still Can't Read is designed to accomplish the following:

1. Increase the awareness that learning disabilities (LD) and Attention-Deficit/Hyperactive Disorder (ADHD) exist in all races, genders, religions, and all socio-economic backgrounds, ranging from the janitor in your local school to the current and former presidents of the United States.
2. Provide resources and services to assist service providers and those who are undiagnosed or diagnosed with LD and/or knows someone who has been.
3. Raise $5 million to provide 1,000 teachers specialized training in five years to become Certified Academic Language Therapists (CALTs) or License Dyslexic Therapists (LDTs) or practitioners so they can learn and apply their understanding of language and literacy resulting in more effective instruction for at-risk students.
4. Utilize research-based reading programs that recognize the nature of dyslexia and related language learning disabilities and the role of multisensory language instruction.
5. Develop a system-wide service delivery model to be implemented with fidelity for (a) the whole school especially struggling minority students; and/or (b) a small group for dyslexic or LD students who are in need of differentiated instruction based on their progress in language or literacy (that is, phoneme awareness, decoding, handwriting, and/or oral language).

6. Write a service delivery model action plan and seek approval by a school or organization's governance that details the following:
   - Buy-in from the parent, teachers, administrators, school, and/or organization governance board
   - The target audience
   - Service delivery models
   - Service capacity
   - The location of services
   - Timely implementation of services
   - Appropriate training for teachers and staff to acquire the necessary competencies and skills
   - Work with other related services located either at the school, other local organizations, or nearby colleges, etc.
   - A budget for either a small, medium, or large public, private, or charter school already on a limited budget

Chapter 1

My Brother's Story

Meet Sammy, My Brother

Everyone has a story about someone they know who's smart in some areas but lacking in others. For some reason, these people just keep messing up. Take a journey along with me as I recall the story of my brother, Sammy. For years, my family and I just couldn't put our finger on how such an articulate and bright young child didn't comprehend like most people. In fact, one friend of mine described Sammy as doing things "bass-ackward." Here is his story.

Sammy was born in Arkansas outside of the city limits of a small country town named Conway. He was a happy and energetic child. He was never bored because he was always doing something to keep himself busy. He was the youngest child of five and thirteen months younger than me. I was called Junior as I was named after our dad. Sammy and I had a close relationship. We did everything together. Our mom always insisted that I watch over and take care of Sammy because I was older. I had the responsibility to take care of Sam. He was special. She saw that Sammy was in a world all of his own. I, however, was just the opposite. It was indeed a challenge for Sammy to be helped by his big brother, who was a compliant child and an outstanding student.

Living in a small country town enabled us to play outside all the time. We created our own games, and Sammy tried to mimic whatever I did. I would skip and run, and Sammy would try to skip and run, but he kept falling. Because Sammy constantly struggled to follow me, he would stop and start crying. When I threw rocks, Sammy would try to do the same thing but without any success because his motor skills were lacking. Merely throwing rocks took him a long time to learn. Once he learned how to throw them, he started throwing them at me because I made everything look so easy while he struggled. Even though Sammy learned how to throw rocks, his arm didn't have the full range of motion necessary for throwing. Therefore, his throwing motion always looked awkward.

Sammy was creative and enjoyed working with his hands. He was a kinesthetic learner. We played games like cowboys and Indians where we'd wear cowboy outfits that we received as Christmas gifts. There were times when Sammy created the bow and arrows for the Indians. If he could touch

1

something, it was easy for him to figure it out and then make it. Sammy also made the slingshots we used to shoot rocks at birds. Our community buzzed about how Sammy could create and fix toys, bicycles, and many other gadgets. Sammy was our neighborhood's modern-day handyman who learned to stick out his chest because he had a sense of accomplishment. He was applauded for his skills that our friends nor I didn't possess. He was in his zone.

We celebrated Sammy outside of the classroom because his challenges from 8 a.m. to 3 p.m. were noticeable during reading and writing classes. During his first few years in school, Sammy's academic struggles were insurmountable. Tasks such as reading one-syllable words and copying words from a book or the blackboard tested his resolve. Often, he transposed letters, such as when writing the word "no" as "on," and transposed numbers such as 3–1 for 1–3. While reading, Sammy would make up substitute words that he memorized, not understanding that reading consisted of viewing each letter as a symbol with a distinct sound blended together. After a while, Sammy became frustrated and couldn't wait for recess, which became his favorite part of school. At recess, he could spend time with his friends, relieving himself of the frustration, anxiety, and tension he experienced in the regular classroom. Sam feared that his teacher would call on him to read or answer a question. He loathed being in the classroom. Unlike some other struggling readers in the class who chose to act out, Sammy never had a behavior problem. He knew that his parents didn't tolerate misbehaving.

Sammy's negative attitude and lack of progress in reading and writing followed him into middle school. Also, it didn't help that I was only a grade above him, allowing the comparisons to follow us from home to school. The adults didn't realize that such comparisons were unfair to both Sammy, who was a struggling student, and me, a straight A student and an obedient child. Sammy's teachers commented that he was "lazy," and he didn't work as hard as me. Our mother constantly berated him when she questioned him for not having homework because I'd been given homework by those same teachers just a year ago. This criticizing and constant comparison diminished Sammy's self-esteem. He felt no one cared about him at school or at home. He was ostracized and convinced he couldn't do anything right. Sammy even tried out for football, but he eventually quit because the coaches ridiculed and scolded him for every mistake, calling him lazy, stupid, and slow. Sammy suffered in silence. He retreated from all activities and eventually people. Because he loved working with his hands, he finally found his niche of drawing. His artwork was unimaginable. Sammy discovered his passion for drawing. A spark rekindled in his eyes, in addition to communication and interaction with his family and friends.

During Sammy's academic battles, I became sensitive to his limitations. I felt his pain. When our mother told me to watch over and take care of Sammy, I took her command literally. I wasn't going to let anybody laugh at, bother, nor embarrass him merely because he couldn't read or write like most kids. In high school, I ensured that Sammy and I had the same class schedule. I saved all my reports and research papers for him to use the following year. Also, I did my homework first, and then I did his. While you may cringe at this idea and call it cheating, I couldn't bear to feel nor see Sammy's frustration, struggling day in and day out to read and write to no avail. I do believe his teachers had a suspicion that I was helping Sammy. He was quiet and stayed focused on drawing in the classroom and never presented any behavior problems in his class or to the teachers. Even during our church's Sunday School class, all the students would turn the pages to read scriptures from the Bible. When it was Sammy's turn to read, I would read for him so that he wouldn't be embarrassed. I'm sure the teacher and other students were curious about what was happening, but no one dared to ask any questions. Sammy's reality was that he was being tortured at school and home, and he felt like he had no place of refuge.

While Sammy had a difficult time with reading and writing the language, he also went through a difficult period with processing information too. For example, Sammy appeared not to get facts straight, and often we thought he wasn't telling the truth. Also, he grappled with following instructions. Those who knew Sammy couldn't understand how a person with a heart of gold would blatantly lie. However, if you didn't know him, you'd think Sammy was a pathological liar. The characteristics of Sammy's learning challenges included the sequencing or the order of events, spatial orientation, and time. Even more devastating was that both he and his teachers had no understanding of his learning challenges or how to provide support or interventions in the classroom. For Sammy, it was easy to make a significant misstep and move on as if nothing had happened.

One time, Sammy and I were horse playing, and part of the game was hitting each other on the arm. Apparently, before the game was over, I'd got the best of Sammy by striking him on his arm, causing a bruise. Several days later, we were both in front of our dad during some family time. Out of nowhere, Sammy reared up and hit me on the arm, knocking me over. Our dad was livid. "Sammy, why did you hit him like that?" Dad asked. Sammy replied, "Leroy hit me first." Dad said that it wasn't what he saw happen.

"Sammy, are you calling me a liar?" Dad asked harshly. Sammy quickly responded by admitting the truth, "Yes, dad." Without thinking, our dad hit Sammy on the arm and knocked him over in his chair just like he did to me. Sammy got up and ran to our mom who immediately came to his rescue. Mom and dad then exchanged unkind words to each other.

I observed this exchange between Sammy and my dad, and then my dad and mom. I couldn't figure out what had just happened. I was dumbfounded when Sammy called our dad a liar. With a startled look on my face, I shook my head in disbelief that someone in their right mind would ever call their dad a liar. While you can undoubtedly think such things, I believe it's likely you'll never act upon those thoughts. I never thought Sammy would be so bold with our dad. I've never seen our mom so enraged when she thought Sammy accused our dad of lying. Our parents have never had a physical fight, but this time they came very close to an all-out fist fight based on Sammy's behavior. What really happened? Did Sammy lie? The answer is no. He didn't lie. In his mind, I'd hit him first. In fact, his memory was blurry at best. I'd hit him first two days before this incident. Yet, all Sammy had focused on was getting even with me no matter if it had transpired today or days ago. He'd locked the prior incident in his mind, and he was going to get revenge no matter when or where. Our dad's question didn't even register with him. As Sammy was experiencing frustration, anxiety, and tension, he didn't process or comprehend the information or the question our dad was asking him.

Sammy also had trouble making sense of what other people said. Our family was experiencing the signs and behavior of Sammy's brain and ears being figuratively miles apart. This disorder is called Auditory Processing Deficiency (APD). (Auditory Processing Disorder n.d.)

When Sammy was in the 8th grade, all his neighborhood classmates had 10-speed bicycles. Because I was working and making money, I purchased us both bicycles. Sammy hadn't saved any of his money, while I had saved about $300. I was able to buy two 10-speed bikes—one red and one green for a total of $200. Our dad picked them up and delivered the bikes to us. Sammy had no idea that I had purchased him a bike. Once he saw the bikes, he was thrilled. He immediately claimed the green one. Our dad told him to hold on and wait. Because I had bought the bikes, Sammy needed to let me choose my bike first. Sammy had an angry outburst and threw a temper tantrum. He yelled that I was always first, and our dad likes me more than him. This assertion was fair. Sammy mumbled angrily underneath his breath so much that you couldn't understand what he said. He cried profusely. Our dad, with his patient demeanor, waited until Sammy calmed down and the tears had vanished. He told us that he was returning the bikes to the store and getting my money back. Sammy was stunned by our dad's decision. Dad finally had his undivided attention, and he took this time to help Sammy see his ungrateful attitude. Dad talked about how I had worked during the summer while Sammy had spent the money he earned on other things. Our dad lectured Sammy about how I showed him kindness by thinking enough of his little brother to buy him a bike so that he wouldn't be the only one in the neighborhood without one. Dad further explained that I thought more highly of others than I did myself. Sammy reluctantly apologized and grabbed the red 10-speed bike. Sammy was ecstatic to have a bike. While his outbursts were unexpected and misunderstood by most people, he wasn't like most people. Due to the manifestation of ADP, he perceived life from a different perspective because he lived in his own world.

Sammy didn't like school, nor did he feel as if his fellow classmates or school teachers liked him. He effectively was operating under their radar and had fallen through the cracks. Sammy was a student with a learning challenge, but he didn't have any disciplinary problems. He was quiet, only existing to spend his time drawing the class time away. Sammy attended school every day. He lived with his two married parents who both were very active in his life. He wasn't from a poor family considered as at-risk due to their living conditions.

Unfortunately, Sammy spent 13 years in school missing out on an enormous amount of basic academics. He walked across the graduation stage and received a diploma that he struggled to read. Sammy hadn't been identified as having a learning disability, and his teachers and school didn't have a prescribed way to work with this population of students.

Living with Abilities

Let's fast forward 40 years in the life of Sammy. When he moved out of our parent's home, he decided to start a new life. He wanted to leave behind all of the negativism of his dyslexia that affected his childhood. Not only did he start a new life, but he also started with a new name. Sammy is now known as Sam. Due to Sam's strong work ethic and entrepreneurial spirit, he will always have a job and make a decent living. He still loves to work with his hands. He likes to buy cars and sell them. A Chevrolet Corvette is one of his toys. He plays with these cars by keeping them well-conditioned and clean. If someone wants his cars more than he does, he will sell it in a New-York second.

Sam lives with my family and me on a five-acre tract of land. In return, Sam takes care of the property and the maintenance of the house. He has his workshop and his barn where he works. Sam is independent and takes good care of himself. Not one time has he mismanaged his money and had to ask me for financial assistance. Sam buys what he wants. When he experiences new challenges that might be over his head, he always has me and my resources nearby to lean on or to walk him through it step-by-step on such things as investments, completing and understanding insurance forms, starting or building businesses, IRS paperwork, interpretation of documents, returning phone calls for him, etc. Sam doesn't have to worry about if I discover he's lacking in reading, his addition is inaccurate, or his comprehension is subpar. He can be himself knowing I accept him as who he is. I'm always ready to assist him.

Despite the challenges Sam may have, I will also hold him accountable. I really believe in winning with accountability. Increased specificity yields decreased miscommunication. Plenty of talking is great but putting it on paper in order of importance is better. Sam gets things done, especially anything that's written down where he can touch and place his hands around it. Now he might draw pictures once he gets it, but at least he has something with which to work.

Sam loves to travel. He's traveled all over Europe. He loves to share all of his positive experiences. At times, it's very challenging for him to follow his flight schedule. At least once a year, he visits his daughter in Denmark. Traveling overseas isn't a simple task for him, and he will admit it publicly. There have been several times when Sam transposed flight numbers and/or departure times. This cost him twice the amount the regular airfare, or at other times, his flight didn't leave until the next day.

For most people, this is unacceptable; however, this is a standard way of life for Sam. For example, I dropped him off at Dallas/Fort Worth International Airport two hours before his departure time. Three days later, I called him to see how he was doing in Denmark. Sam said he was doing great, but that he'd just arrived in Denmark. The first thing that I thought was how could that be? I asked Sam again to make sure he had understood my questions correctly. Sam concurred, and then he went on to explain his plight. The interesting thing about flying from one city to another city is you must have a boarding pass, which comes in a different format depending on the carrier. Certain parts of the boarding pass are self-explanatory, like the customer's name, your departure/destination location, and the airline. Other parts of the boarding pass can be somewhat confusing, like the flight, date, departure time, gate, boarding time, zone, and seat number. If you notice, the first part of the boarding pass is alphanumeric, while the second part is mostly numeric. When Sam first looked at his boarding pass, he saw the departure time as 1:30 and the flight number as 1110. Therefore, he had me to drop him off at the airport two hours early for his international flight. Once Sam went to check in, he had missed his flight. Sam was stunned because he knew he was early for his Denmark trip. The agent looked at his boarding pass and immediately saw the problem. His departure time was 11:10, and the flight number was 130. Sam had switched the departure time and the flight number. This mistake cost Sam time and money. Flights to Denmark aren't very frequent; therefore, Sam spent almost 24 hours at the DFW Airport until the next flight two days later. It also cost him nearly an extra $1,000 to rebook his flight.

According to Sam, incidents like this have happened before. It's not something he likes to talk about. In fact, I'm sure Sam will go the extra mile to cover up the times his dyslexia has interfered with his life. Sam and I have a very close relationship. I've seen the ongoing effects of dyslexia baring down on him both personally and professionally. However, because I am aware of his dyslexic behaviors, I have helped him navigate mistakes with a softer landing, whereas it could've been devastating. When the milk is out of the carton, it's too late to put it back in. There's no reason to cry over spilled milk. It's a way of life together. I always help Sam to see the glass as half full instead of half empty. I have helped him learn how to become a winner even in a losing situation.

Most people cannot even imagine living in a world where something that seems so simple to one person is very complicated to another person, such as the spatial orientation of numbers or the transposition of numbers. This type of occurrence isn't just related to traveling to Denmark, it's an everyday part of life for some. If the truth is told, I likely wouldn't have known about Sam's ordeal if I hadn't taken him to the airport, then called him three days later to check on him.

This is Sam's story. It takes a brave man to come out and share his story even when it seems embarrassing for the whole world to know. Sam isn't only a brave man, but he's my hero. It's is because of his dyslexia that I've been able to help thousands of students and parents, as well as find my true meaning and purpose in life. In fact, my life is now purpose-driven because of Sam.

The Real Issue

Our school systems are not equipped to work with learning-challenged students. These students eventually fall through the cracks, with some ending up in our penal systems. How can a student who attends school almost every day for 13 years struggle to read and write? How can a student like Sammy who builds, draws, paints, and expresses himself artistically have such a difficult time expressing himself verbally or even struggle with reading?

Is it the school's fault or the parents? Or is it the fault of an educational system that's broken with no interventions for various learning styles or the untrained or insensitive teachers who work with students with APD, ADHD, dyslexia, etc.? The real issue is that our school systems aren't equipped to work with students who have cognitive problems. If our school systems continue to ignore or sweep these severe educational issues under the rug, they continue to push these unprepared students out of school lacking an appropriate education. Such a disservice may likely eventually lead them to crime and the penal systems.

This problem of being ill-equipped doesn't just exist at Sammy's school. It exists in schools scattered across our nation. Our politicians keep coming up with catchy new slogans such as "No Child Left Behind," yet the reality is that some American children are being left behind while everyone is pointing fingers and playing the blame game. Parents are blaming the schools, and the schools are blaming the parents. Unfortunately, the majority of these students are male and children of color, just like Sammy. Are students with learning challenges being discriminated against or is this blatant racism? Despite the reason or who's to blame, the bottom line is that Sammy still can't read.

In summary, as of 2018, I'm still the only African-American male CALT in the country. Our needs are too great in the minority community for this to still hold true, especially with such large populations of boys located in inner cities. There just is no excuse. Change must happen. I firmly believe that I must be part of the solution. It's up to me to propel all communities to help stamp out illiteracy in this country. No more excuses for Why Sammy Still Can't Read.

We as American citizens must look at illiteracy as a crisis. This issue will never become a priority unless our parents of children with learning disabilities fully understands and becomes their child advocates and force our school systems and politicians to make this part of their agenda while running for office. It might take a candidate with a personal interest like a child in the public school system with a learning disability to affect changes nationwide. This is not about black nor white, have and have not. This is about all children exercising their civil rights so that no child will be left behind.

Chapter 2

A Man on a Mission

Remain Focused

Time was ticking slowly away. Life was passing me by. I felt an urgent prompting in my heart to put down the television remote and eliminate the humdrum routine of work and play. With depleted energy levels due to the day in and day out of life's challenges, I needed to see and experience small victories daily for me to remain focused.

This was not an easy task. I had to develop a stick-to-it mentality in order not to lose my grip on my vision. Author and speaker John C. Maxwell, in The 15 Invaluable Laws of Growth book, wrote, "You will never change your life until you change something you do daily." (Maxwell 2014) "Small disciplines repeated with consistency every day lead to great achievements gained slowly over time." The courage to stay focused on the vision was threefold—discipline, exercise, and a renewed mind.

The moment you see your vision on the horizon, temptations and distractions continue to increase. In June 1995 my vision became a reality. At that time, I met one of one of the most beautiful, articulate, and well-spoken young woman I've ever met. She was a grant writer, and public relations consultant focused on her own goals. I told her about my vision and asked if she would consider working with me to enhance and extend God's kingdom. Within a few weeks, we began working together and enjoying each other's company. We prayed every time we were together, asking God to take captive any forms of temptation so that we could complete our work.

Being self-disciplined was the only way to obtain my vision. However, the newly hired grant writer was destined to be more than a business partner, and I told her that I loved her just weeks after just working together. She had no response to that at the time, as she likely was more focused than me. I firmly believe that to accomplish the things that you've not obtained, you must make sacrifices. I believe there's a higher calling that all of us must answer to, and the only thing to do is to keep our eyes focused on the vision.

The Art of Discipline

Deeply embedded in my heart, mind, and actions are the verses about vision from the writers of the Bible books of Proverbs and Habakkuk. Proverbs

29:18 says, "Without knowledge, people perish, and without a vision, people perish." Habakkuk 2:2 takes it even further. "Write the vision down, and it will come to past." (NIV 2011) These verses became my marching orders to the point that people thought I was insane. I didn't buy into this thinking. I honestly believed that insanity is when you keep doing the same things expecting to get different results. I am now disciplined and focused with a new vision.

Research proves that only 1 percent of the world's population is considered to be successful in their field or wealth. So why is less than 1 percent of the world's population considered to be successful and wealthy? (Hardoon 2015) You must pay a steep price to be the boss. It takes discipline. Merriam-Webster's Dictionary defines discipline as "training that corrects, molds, or perfects the mental faculties or moral characters." (Merriam-Webster.com n.d.) Usually, the number-one trait of a wealthy person is discipline because it requires that something most people will not do. When I had the vision to start FOCUS Centre of Learning, Inc., it was during a season of living in the fiery furnace of struggle and correction, as I was shaping my character, molding and sharpening my mental capacity.

Exercise–No Pain, No Gain

I reminded myself every day that to be successful, I needed discipline and exercise, and to renew my mind by reading positive literature and laying aside any things that could lead to temptation. By being obedient in these things daily, I knew I was one step closer to accomplishing my vision. The next step was exercise, which enabled me to see physically that my vision was obtainable if I persevered daily. While I was growing up, I was only a basketball player and didn't participate in any other athletics; therefore, lifting weights and bodybuilding was foreign to me.

In the late 1980s, I was able only to do five push-ups, whereas most athletes were able to do 15 or 20. My goal was to do 1,000 push-ups and 1,000 sit-ups daily. Accomplishing this would seem to be an impossible goal if you are only doing five per day. I was determined, however, to do the seemingly impossible, which helped me to realize that I could do what it takes to run a successful business. After two weeks, I was doing ten push-ups nonstop, five times a day. In four months, I was doing 50 push-ups nonstop, five times a day, equaling 250 push-ups daily. After one year, I could do 100 pushups nonstop, ten times a day, reaching my goal of 1,000 push-ups per day. Did this happen overnight? No. Was it very challenging? Yes. Did I achieve my goal? Yes. Often, people want something for nothing without paying the price, and we want to be an overnight success. When our plans or goals don't materialize, we tend to blame it on someone else.

The race isn't giving to the swift nor the strong, but to the one that perseveres. (NIV 2011) I remember many times my body was breaking down for one reason or another with bursitis and other ailments, but I stayed focused on the goal and accepted no excuses. Besides, I accomplished my goal for the sit-ups, which was more obtainable when compared to the push-ups. After achieving one goal, I wanted to get to the gym and lift weights, something I'd never done before. My goal was to have a buffed physique and to have the best-trained body at the age of 35. I gave myself four to five years to accomplish this goal. I had no idea what I was getting myself into with this weight-lifting goal. However, one thing I knew for sure was that once I accomplished my goal, I would be one step closer to achieving my vision of having a successful school.

Because I had a hectic schedule for work, it was almost impossible to find time to work out at the gym. I worked at a private school from 7:30 a.m. to 4 p.m. I also worked as a CALT with private students from 4:30 p.m. to 9:30 p.m. most weekdays. Because of a lack of time in my schedule, I went to the gym at 3:30 a.m. Yes, it was challenging, but I had to stay focused on my ultimate goal. To me, it was another discipline in training my physical and mental faculties for my central vision. Many of us likely don't know many successful people because most of society isn't willing to go put in that extra effort to be successful. Yes, they have the desire, but they're not prepared to pay the ultimate price. How many times did I tell myself that I must be crazy for going in at 3 a.m. and that I was going to skip that day? Too many. However, I also knew that if I didn't work out, I wouldn't accomplish my vision. I was driven and disciplined.

I was almost 35 years old when I reached my goal of having a buffed physique. I received numerous compliments from colleagues, friends, family, and strangers. Obtaining and keeping my body in shape is a matter of discipline. I believe in Philippians 4:13, "I can do all things through Christ that strengthens me." (NIV 2011) I didn't need my ego massaged, nor did I get the big head, but occasionally I would stick out my chest and tell myself that I was one step closer to accomplishing the vision.

Renewing My Mind, The Staying Point

"Do not be conformed by the things of this world but be transformed by the renewing of your mind," as the Apostle Paul wrote in Romans 12:1– 2. (NIV

2011) The mind is too valuable to waste by putting junk in it. Many times, you have to remove yourself from watching television and do something productive. I consistently read many books that affected my thought patterns and my actions. Out of all the great books, the one that has influenced me the most is the Bible. Every day I wouldn't only read the Bible, but I felt I was called to action daily to go out and make the world a better place. I knew that the Bible would order my steps as I make my plans so that the moral character developed in me would be my greatest asset as I worked toward my vision. I learned to love the unlovable, to forgive the unforgivable, to reach the unreachable, and to teach the unteachable. I discovered there was a unique calling on my life to do the impossible so that many lives would be changed and enable people to impact the future of our world. No, I didn't know how it would unfold, and often my vision became so big that fear would set in. I knew I would be walking into unchartered territory, but I also knew from my daily reading that wherever I went, I wouldn't be alone because it's a faith walk. I reminded myself that faith without action is dead. I also knew others were consistently examining my actions, and my foundation of moral character would direct my path to success. Pleasing God without faith is impossible. Faith and fear cannot reside in the same place. Fear is the work of the enemy. Fear is false evidence appearing real.

As I read the Bible on a daily basis, I discovered the truth about my life and why I was born. First of all, it's not about me, but how I have been used in this world as a vessel to make a difference. My life is not only about how I live but also how I give. The greatest blessing for me is not to receive, but to give. I am blessed to be a blessing to others. I am the voice for the poorly educated. I am the voice for the learning disabled. I am the voice for the disenfranchised. Winston Churchill once said, "Occasionally, a man will stumble over the truth, but most men will pick themselves up and hurry on as if nothing has happened." (quoteinvestigator.com 2012) As you see, I'm not like most men. As I read my favorite book, the Bible, I've been called to speak and carry out the truth, so that many children and parents could be set free from the disease called illiteracy.

As I trained my body for years working out in the gym and trained my mind by reading the Bible, I have remained focused on my vision despite the many trials and adversities I had to face and overcome. As I faced the trials, I relied on James 1:2-4, which says "the testing of your faith produces perseverance," which enabled me to become "more mature, and complete, not lacking anything." (NIV 2011) My focus was my vision, and now my vision is my FOCUS, which stands for Focus on Children in

United States. Because of the art of discipline, I founded the Centre, which then created and established the school aptly named FOCUS Learning Academy, designed to serve 75 percent of students with a learning disability or reading struggles.

A Focused Vision

My vision finally had become a reality. I could begin to ensure that America's children could learn to read, train teachers with the right programs to effectively teach the struggling reader, and eventually launch training centers and various schools throughout this country. In the meantime, however, as a society we need to fix our school's educational system to embrace and help all children, no matter their race, creed, religion, disability, or gender.

Education reform has been the most talked about subject in the last four decades. Despite adversity, I spent 30 years of my life educating myself about learning disabilities after discovering why Sammy graduated from public school with a diploma that he had a difficult time reading. This discovery inspired me to become a man on a mission! I felt that the educational system was helping LD students; however, I knew they needed to treat this disorder like a doctor would treat cancer. It's mission-critical to fight intentionally and strategically to prevent our public-school systems from becoming a cancerous educational system. These students needed to be timely identified, properly diagnosed, and appropriately remediated so they would not be forced to drop out of school.

I had a clear vision to stand up for these students, so they wouldn't be sentenced to a long, drawn-out death of despair, spiraling downward into the prison system or an early grave. I wasn't going to sit back and watch these children become a statistic, nor would I recline in my rocking chair while watching most talk shows ridicule uneducated African Americans. It was time out for the nation's top education reform agendas to use this as a mere item on their check-off list or given just a minor mention in the last five presidential candidate's election platforms.

Breaking the Link of Illiteracy

After months of soul-searching, praying and reflecting on Sammy's past educational woes, the light bulb finally went off. It costs less to send a child to Yale than to send a child to jail. I stumbled across the truth. There is a direct correlation between African-American males and students with learning disabilities in the penal system who cannot read.

Failure to address learning and attention issues too often leads to students being incarcerated, which further disrupts their education and contributes to high dropout and recidivism rates. Some studies indicate a third or more of incarcerated youth have learning disabilities, and an even higher proportion may show signs of ADHD.

A Study of Juvenile Justice Schools in the south and the nation reported that "the most disadvantaged, troubled students in the south and the nation attend schools in the juvenile justice systems. These children, mostly teenagers, usually are behind in school, possess substantial learning disabilities, exhibit recognizable behavioral problems, and are coping with serious emotional or psychological problems. They are often further behind and hampered with more personal problems than any other identifiable group of students in the nation's elementary and secondary schools. Very often they are confined in large, overly restrictive institutional facilities that are operated without priority or focus on their education." (Suits, Dunn and Sabree 2014) Steven Klein of the U.S. Dept. of Education writes, "American prisoners have consistently tested at the lowest levels of educational achievement, and at the highest levels of illiteracy and educational disability of any segment in our society." The effect of prison education programs on recidivism. He and his colleagues conclude, "considering the vast numbers of inmates that do not possess the basic social and educational skills that they need to function in society, it should come as no surprise that many of those released from prison or jail will eventually return." (Esperian 2010)

Test results from the juvenile justice schools own federal reports provide additional supporting evidence. In 2008-09, roughly two-thirds of all students in the South and the nation who were tested as they entered state juvenile residential institutions were behind grade level in reading and in math. In local juvenile institutions, below-grade rates in reading were 42 percent in the South and 44 percent throughout the nation. (Suits, Dunn and Sabree 2014)

The Literacy Project Foundation found that three out of five people in U.S. prisons and 85 percent of juvenile offenders have trouble reading. Other research has estimated that illiteracy rates in prisons are as high as 75 percent of the prison population. This unaddressed issue in the United States' prison system is inextricably linked to high recidivism rates. This unaddressed issue in the United States' prison system is inextricably linked to high recidivism rates. (Sainato 2017) While I was alarmed by this research, the reality-- illiteracy is a significant problem in our society.

Based on many studies on prison education programs contend that a comprehensive educational program could make a significant contribution toward reducing the educational deficiencies experienced by many in the nation's incarcerated population. An educational program, in turn, could have a positive impact on the many other social problems facing these individuals. It's especially crucial that programs incorporate literacy instruction into the educational services of prisons. One of the fundamental skills for inmate training programs is literacy. Research, however, contends that if appropriately managed, education, employment, and resocialization programs can work toward reducing recidivism rates. If these programs are adequately operated and have the desired effects, it justifies the positive cost outcomes.

A report from the U.S. Departments of Education and Justice suggest that "reforming and improving education programs in juvenile justice secure care settings to provide committed youths with high-quality instruction and supportive services comparable to those provided to students in community schools represents a monumental step forward for our nation's juvenile justice system." (U.S. Departments of Education and Justice, Guiding Principles for Providing High-Quality Education in Juvenile Justice Secure Care Settings 2014)

In summary, I needed the alignment of spiritual, emotional, and physical aspects of my life to be intact. With renewed energy, I was on a new educational mission. I was on a quest to find a solution for students like my brother Sam and to help reduce high illiteracy rates and reading issues due to an undiagnosed or diagnosed learning disability. It was time for me to stand up and put my training as a Certified Academic Language Therapist to use by providing a viable educational option for parents, students, teachers, and school administrators. I began the process of creating an awareness campaign in the African-American community that we have serious reading challenges as deadly as the malignant cancerous cells in the body. If the academic problems are left undiagnosed or untreated like the cancerous cell growth in the body, students will either drop out of school, end up in the penal system, drain the welfare system and ultimately live without any hope.

Chapter 3
Diagnosing the Problem

Behind the braided hairstyle, quiet and gentle demeanor, nine-year-old Marion Apipah is articulate and bright. She hopes to become an archaeologist. Erica Williamson, 14, is sensitive with a strong will and an outstanding speaker. Both girls are intuitive and excel with hands-on learning—a kinesthetic learning style.

These two bright and intelligent African-American young ladies both possessed strong reasoning powers in addition to gifts with spoken language and high creativity, yet they struggled with learning to read, write, and spell. They both suffered in a world of constant humiliation because they had difficulty in figuring out how to translate patterns on a page into words, thoughts, and ideas. Both parents were in crisis due to the girl's misunderstanding of symbols, issues with processing information, and their inability to read created tension, anxiety, and frustration.

Through years of frustration, Marion's parent, a psychologist, and Erica's mom, a lawyer, realized that their daughter's learning challenges were not normal when compared to their overall intelligence. They felt that their children didn't possess the enhanced language and literary experiences required to progress at the same rate as their classmates. The Texas Scottish Rite Hospital for Children tested Marion at the age of 8 and Erica at the age of 11. Both girls were dyslexic.

In our educational system, we've created excuses, such as we can't ask our teachers to do more than what they are trained or get paid to do. Most teachers are only adequately prepared to teach general education students and not students with learning disabilities. If we believe that all children can learn, then are we leaving 1 out of 5 students who have a learning disability behind? In most cases, an 80 percent success rate for a classroom teacher isn't bad; however, it is the contrary for the parents of the 20% of students who have a learning disability. (Horowitz, Rawe and Whittaker 2017) Who is paying attention or doing something about the underlying problem for the struggling students?

Some researchers contend that teachers lack sufficient coursework to teach students with learning disabilities. One study suggests that while university programs may dedicate some coursework and time to addressing the basic and fundamental facts on students with disabilities and the practice of inclusion, many feel that this is insufficient in creating teachers who will be able to meet successfully the needs of their inclusive students. "Although 7 out of 10 surveyed pre-service teachers stated that they were required to take a special education course during their preparation program, 100% of these teachers reported that this requirement was satisfied by only 3-6 credit hours out of a total of 3,942 hours. Participants also described these classes as being basic, introductory courses that did little other than briefly introduce the fundamentals of federal law and its relationship to special needs children," according to a 2009 NERA Conference Proceedings document. (Rosenzweig 2009)

If we truly believe that all children can learn, then our children must be taught by a teacher who has specialized training to work with struggling readers and those who can't sit still in their seats due to hyperactivity. A diagnosis, interventions and long-term strategies are essential for struggling readers. Finding interventions for a struggling reader is no different than intervening if a child has sores on their head or some other type of illness.

Unlike education, trained specialists exist in every aspect of life. You may be wondering; can this be true? Yes, really! You need to see the right doctor to diagnose illnesses or diseases. Let's take a look at specialists who can diagnose and provide medical treatment plans that we can trust to handle our problems. (Clark 2014)

- Cardiologist: Specializes in the treatment of the heart and any related diseases
- Obstetrician/gynecologist: Specializes in the care of the female reproductive system, also, delivering those precious children who may or may not have a learning disability
- Oncologist: Specializes in working with cancer patients to provide an accurate diagnosis and a treatment plan
- Orthodontist: Specializes in working with the teeth, gums, and most other aspects of the mouth
- Neonatologist: Specializes in the care of newborn infants to ensure their successful entry into a healthy life
- Neurologist: Specializes in the treatment of diseases and ailments related to the human brain and determines the causes and the treatment of such illness as Alzheimer's, Parkinson, Dementia, among many others

- Pediatrician: Specializes in the care of infants, children, and young adolescents from 1 to 18 years of age
- Podiatrist: Specializes in identifying and treating issues related to the feet and ankles
- Radiologist: Specializes in diagnosing and detecting physiological ailments using X-rays and other imaging technologies
- Surgeon: Specializes in performing a variety of surgeries on the body

I believe you can see the big picture here. The real issues are as follows:

- Children who can't read due to a lack of exposure to formal education, may have the characteristics of LD, dyslexia, ADHD, APD, etc.
- These overlooked children need special programs that explicitly teach them to read and a trained person to facilitate this need.

Like the medical professions previously listed, a prescribed method and a trained specialist is needed to implement the treatment and intervention for a struggling reader. Currently, there's a massive need for adults to have a passion for teaching specific reading programs, a nurturing personality, and understands the importance of using prescriptive teaching methods for the population of struggling readers. There must be a clear understanding that reading is fundamental, and our children are free when they learn to read. Like my friend, Phyllis Hunter, once said to me, "reading is the new civil right." (Hunter 2012)

Understanding Learning Disorders

In the average public K–12 school classroom, most teachers view students like Marion and Erica negatively. Their verbal reading levels fall far below prediction for their quick and alert intelligence. Learning and attention issues are far more common than many people think, affecting 1 in 5 children. (Horowitz, Rawe and Whittaker 2017) With supportive policies and increased awareness among parents, educators, and communities, these students can thrive academically, socially, and emotionally.

Dyslexia and other learning disabilities are lifelong challenges. There are no cures or quick fixes. Because their parents could afford private school tuition, Marion attended a moderately inexpensive private school, while Erica's parents spent about $9,000 annually to ensure she could read, write, and spell. Today, the girls attend a far North Dallas private school specializing in the treatment of children with learning disabilities such as dyslexia and ADHD. Intensive language therapy also enhances their daily learning with trained CALTs. Both girls suffer from a learning disability and are at-risk of failure if appropriate remediation isn't available to them.

Research from various organizations shows there are at least 70 symptoms that appear to be related to a variety of learning disabilities categories. (The State of LD: Understanding Learning and Attention Issues 2018) If a child suffers from any condition that inhibits natural learning, it can fall under one of these categories. This chapter explores the definition, signs, symptoms, and treatment for the 13 categories of disabilities. (Dragoo 2017). Behaviors, methods and programs are presented through the lens of traditional public schools, non-traditional charter schools and youth organizations for possible ways to offer long-term care for students with disabilities. Let's look at the given facts surrounding disabilities.

In 2015–16, the number of students ages 3–21 receiving special education services was 6.7 million, or 13 percent of all public school students. In the public schools, 34 percent had specific learning disabilities. (McFarland, et al. 2018)

Special education programs are specifically designed for students identified as having various disabilities that affect learning, and physical, sensory, or emotional development. While there are 13 special education categories listed in the federal special education law, i.e., *Individuals with Disabilities Education Improvement Act of 2004 (IDEA)*, figures from the U.S. Department of Education suggest that specific learning disability, speech/language impairment, and mental retardation are the largest disability categories for SLD students. (Truth in Labeling: Disproportionality in Special Education 2007)

13 Categories of a Disability

Under the Federal Law
Individuals with Disabilities Education Act (IDEA)

1 Specific Learning Disability (SLD)

The umbrella term *SLD* covers a specific group of learning issues that affect a child's ability to read, write, listen, speak, reason, or do math. Some issues that could fall in this group are Dyslexia, Dysgraphia, Dyscalculia, Auditory Processing Disorder, and Nonverbal Learning Disabilities.

2 Other Health Impairment

The umbrella phrase other health impairment covers conditions that limit a child's strength, energy, or alertness. One example is an attention issue such as ADHD.

3 Autism Spectrum Disorder (ASD)

ASD is a developmental disability and covers a wide range of symptoms and skills, but mainly refers to those that affect a child's social and communication skills. ASD can also impact their behavior.

4 Emotional Disturbance

Children covered under the phrase emotional disturbance can have several mental disorders, including Anxiety Disorder, Schizophrenia, Bipolar Disorder, Obsessive-Compulsive Disorder, and Depression.

5 Speech or Language Impairment

The umbrella phrase speech or language impairment covers several communication problems, including Stuttering, Impaired Articulation, Language Impairment, or Voice Impairment.

6 Visual Impairment, Including Blindness

A child who has vision problems is considered to have a Visual Impairment. This condition includes both partial sight and blindness. If eyewear can correct a vision problem, then it doesn't qualify.

7 Deafness

Children with a diagnosis of Deafness have a severe hearing impairment. They can't process language through hearing.

8 Hearing Impairment

The phrase hearing impairment refers to a hearing loss not covered by the definition of Deafness. This type of loss can change or fluctuate over time. Being hard of hearing isn't the same as having an Auditory Processing Disorder.

9 Deaf-Blindness

Children with a diagnosis of Deaf-Blindness have both Hearing and Visual Impairments. Their communication and other needs are so great that programs for the deaf or blind can't meet them.

10 Orthopedic Impairment

Any impairment to a child's body, no matter what the cause, is considered an Orthopedic Impairment. One example is cerebral palsy, a condition caused by damage to areas of the brain that control the body.

11 Intellectual Disability

Children with Intellectual Disability have below-average intellectual ability. They can also have poor communication, self-care, and social skills. Down Syndrome is one example of an intellectual disability.

12 Traumatic Brain Injury

Traumatic Brain Injury is defined as a brain injury caused by an accident or some kind of physical force.

13 Multiple Disabilities

A child with Multiple Disabilities has more than one condition covered by IDEA. Having multiple issues creates educational needs that can't be met in a program for any one condition.

From 2011-2015, the percentage of the population ages 12 through 17 served under Part B increased gradually from 10.8 percent to 11.3 percent. In 2015, the most prevalent disability category of students ages 6 through 21 served under IDEA, Part B, was specific learning disability (specifically, 2,348,891, or 38.8 percent, of the 6,050,725 students ages 6 through 21 served under Part B). The next most common disability category was speech or language impairment (17.3 percent), followed by other health impairment (15.0 percent), autism (9.1 percent), intellectual disability (6.9 percent), and emotional disturbance (5.7 percent). Students ages 6 through 21 in "Other disabilities combined" accounted for the remaining 7.2 percent of students ages 6 through 21 served under IDEA, Part B. (39th Annual Report to Congress 2017)

Learning Disabilities (LD)—The Facts

Would you spend your time criticizing or blaming a blind man because of his inability to see or walk straight like you? If so, you would be punishing him for his disability, which is a violation of the laws of the American Disabilities Act. Because of his disability, it's likely you would be more compassionate and understanding of a disorder, rather than offer merciless comments about his behavior. (Laws & Guidance Civil Rights: Disability Discrimination 2012)

Learning disabilities are both real and permanent. Research shows that learning disabilities arise from neurological differences found in the brain's structure and function, which affect a person's ability to receive, store, process, retrieve, or communicate information. The most common types of specific learning disabilities are those impacting the areas of reading, math, and written expression. They can co-occur with other attention, language, and behavior disorders but are distinct in how they impact learning.

Children with learning and attention issues are as smart as their peers, and if provided the right support, can achieve at high levels. However, thousands of poor inner-city African-American males and females continue to battle learning and attention issues daily without proper diagnosis and interventions. An estimated 20 percent of the student population has difficulty with the symbols of written language, including reading, reading comprehension, writing, and spelling. (Horowitz, Rawe and Whittaker 2017) As a result, these students can't master the English language. Therefore, they cannot read and pass state standardized test, or score high on national tests such as the SAT and ACT. Often, these children are placed in special education, drop out of school, or receive low grades if they remain in the standard classroom. It ultimately affects their self-esteem, causing other issues to surface soon.

What Is a Learning Disability (LD)?

For the school-aged population, the most commonly used definition for such learning and attention issues are in the federal special education law titled the Individuals with Disabilities Education Act (IDEA). (Disabilities, Types of Learning Disabilities n.d.) IDEA terms it as a specific learning disability (SLD). According to IDEA, SLD is

> a disorder in one or more of the basic psychological processes involved in understanding or in using language, spoken or written, which disorder may manifest itself in the imperfect ability to listen, think, speak, read, write, spell, or do mathematical calculations.
>
> such term includes such conditions as perceptual disabilities, brain injury, minimal brain dysfunction, dyslexia, and developmental aphasia.
>
> such term does not include a learning problem that is primarily the result of visual, hearing, or motor disabilities, of mental retardation*, of emotional disturbance, or of environmental, cultural, or economic disadvantage.

—20 U.S.C. § 1401 (30) *Now known as intellectual disability.
(Horowitz, Rawe and Whittaker 2017)

Learning disabilities interfere with learning the basic skills of reading, writing and math. They are neurologically based processing problems. They can also interfere with higher-level skills such as organization, time planning, abstract reasoning, long- or short-term memory, and attention. It's important to realize that learning disabilities can affect an individual's life beyond academics and impact relationships with family, friends, and others in the workplace.

LD shouldn't be confused with learning problems, which are primarily the result of visual, hearing, or motor handicaps; of mental retardation; of emotional disturbance; or of environmental, cultural, or economic disadvantages. Learning and attention issues aren't the result of low intelligence, poor vision or hearing, or the lack of access to quality instruction. (Horowitz, Rawe and Whittaker 2017)

Common Types of Specific Learning Disabilities (LD)

The most common types of specific learning disabilities (LD) are those impacting the areas of reading, math, and written expression. They can co-occur with other attention, language, and behavior disorders, but they're distinct in how they impact learning. Learning Disabilities or LD is an umbrella phrase describing several other more specific learning disabilities.

The common examples of learning disabilities are dyslexia, dyscalculia, and dysgraphia. Other difficulties that affect learning and behavior include ADHD, Executive function deficit, dyspraxia, and Nonverbal learning disabilities. These examples of learning difficulties do not discriminate. They cross all racial, ethic, socio-economics, gender, professions/occupations whether unemployed/employed. A more detailed description of the learning disabilities including characteristics, signs and symptoms, and treatment options are found in this chapter.

Changing Public Perception

This book, Why Sammy Still Can't Read, is intended to help parents, educators, students, and the community-at-large to understand learning disabilities and to eradicate the looming stigma associated with LD. While progress is slow in the awareness phase, researchers are in high pursuit of fact finding and information sharing to help dispel rumors with publishing more scientific-based studies. For example, the Emily Hall Tremaine Foundation commissioned the fourth in a series of GFK Roper studies to examine the public's attitudes about LD. The 2010 report captured the understanding and attitudes of the public and of educators, and offered data to assess progress —

or lack of progress — in how both parents and the United States educational system are addressing the needs of children who learn differently. (Cortiella and Horowitz 2014)

The 2010 GFK Roper study found that:

- A majority of the general public and educators in the U.S. agree that children learn in different ways. Eight in 10 Americans (79 percent, a value that is up nine points from 2004) agree (strongly/somewhat) that children learn in different ways. Virtually all educators (99 percent) say the same.
- The number of Americans who say they are familiar with learning disabilities is on the rise. In 2010, members of the general public were much more likely to say that they have heard or read "a lot" about learning disabilities than in both 2004 and 1999.
- The majority of the general public recognizes the fact that children with learning disabilities are of average or above-average intelligence. Eight in 10 Americans (80 percent) consider the statement "children with learning disabilities are just as smart as you and me" to be accurate.
- Almost all parents (96 percent) today agree that children can learn to compensate for a learning disability with proper instruction.

The 2010 study found that both the general public and parents, as well as educators, increasingly embrace the foundational notion that individuals with LD have unique learning needs and challenges and that their ability to achieve is not due to factors such as below-average intelligence. LD affects rich, poor, young, or old. In fact, many learning disabled high-profile people have overcome their challenges and chose to serve as advocates to shed light on learning disorders.

Several publications have reported that former President George W. Bush has dyslexia. According to a *Vanity Fair* article, Bush has problems with pronouncing words and using them in a sentence structure. During his childhood, he used over 5,000 flashcards with words written on them to memorize words to try to overcome this weakness. "This explains a lot!" Speaker of the House Nancy Pelosi remarked when she learned of the president's disability. (UnNews: Bush admits to being dyslexic 2008) Other notable leaders, entertainers, and athletes who are dyslexic include Whoopi Goldberg, Danny Glover, Cher, Winston Churchill, Nolan Ryan, and Nelson Rockefeller. (Famous People with Dyslexia 2011) A more in-depth look at the lives of these individuals are in Chapter 8.

Characteristics of Learning Disabilities

People with LD have average or above-average intelligence. A discrepancy between an LD individual's IQ and actual achievement also exists. As a result, learning disabilities are referred to as hidden disabilities because the person looks perfectly normal and possibly a very bright and intelligent person, yet they may be unable to demonstrate the skill levels expected for someone similar to their age.

Because difficulties with reading, writing, and math are recognizable problems during the school years, students can receive a formal evaluation if they exhibit the characteristics of learning disabilities during that time. However, some individuals don't receive any evaluation until they are in post-secondary education or as adults in the workforce. Other individuals with learning disabilities may never receive an evaluation and go through life never knowing why they're having academic difficulties and problems in their jobs or relationships.

Regardless of a person's status, more awareness about LD is needed. Research shows that parents and educators still are confused and have an immense lack of knowledge about learning disabilities. A further examination of accurate information ranging from definitions, causes, characteristics, to treatment will assist parents and educators of young children in successfully understanding and coping with LD follows in the next section.

Dyslexia

Research shows that dyslexia is perhaps the most widely known learning disability. Dyslexia is referred to as a Language-Based Learning Disability. Dyslexia is well-recognized of the subtypes of specific learning disabilities, overwhelming difficulty affecting reading, writing, spelling, and related language-based processing skills in ordinarily intelligent children who have proper education and instructional opportunities in school and at home. The severity of this specific learning disability can differ in among individuals, and it can affect reading fluency, decoding, reading comprehension, recall, and sometimes speech. Also, it can exist along with other related disorders. If a child has no financial resources to help them, they usually fall by the wayside—dropping out of school and some may end up going to prison. Let's check out further signs and symptoms of learning disabilities. (Disabilities, Types of Learning Disabilities n.d., Cortiella and Horowitz 2014)

Signs and Symptoms

- Has difficulty with phonemic awareness (i.e., the ability to notice, think about, and work with individual word sounds)
- Has issues with phonological processing (i.e., detecting and discriminating differences in phonemes or speech sounds)
- Has difficulties with word decoding, fluency, the rate of reading, rhyming, spelling, vocabulary, comprehension, and written expression
- Reads slowly and painfully
- Experiences decoding errors, especially with the order of letters
- Shows a wide disparity between listening comprehension and reading comprehension of some text
- Has trouble spelling
- Has possible difficulty with handwriting
- Exhibits difficulty recalling known words
- Has difficulty with written language
- Can have trouble with math computations
- Decoding real words is easier than nonsense words
- Substitutes one small sight words for another: a, I, he, the, there, was

Strategies

- Provide a quiet area for activities such as reading and answering comprehension questions
- Use books on tape
- Use books with large print and large spacing between lines
- Provide a copy of the lecture notes
- Do not count spelling on history, science, or other similar tests
- Allow alternative forms of book reports
- Allow the use of a laptop or other computers for in-class essays
- Use multisensory teaching methods
- Teach students to use logic rather than rote memory
- Present materials in small units

Dysgraphia

Dysgraphia affects a person's handwriting ability and fine motor skills. A person with dysgraphia can have problems including illegible handwriting, inconsistent spacing, poor spatial planning on paper, poor spelling, and difficult composing their writing, as well as thinking and writing at the same time. (Disabilities, Types of Learning Disabilities n.d., Cortiella and Horowitz 2014)

Signs and Symptoms

- Tight and awkward pencil grip and body position
- Tires quickly while writing and avoids writing or drawing tasks
- Has trouble forming letter shapes, in addition to adding inconsistent spacing between letters or words
- Has difficulty writing or drawing on a line or within margins
- Has issues with organizing their thoughts on paper
- Can't keeping track of thoughts that are already written down
- Has difficulty with syntax structure and grammar
- Experiences a large gap between their written ideas and understanding as demonstrated through their speech
- Can have illegible printing and cursive writing, despite the appropriate time and attention given to the task
- Shows inconsistencies in mixtures of print and cursive letters; upper- and lowercase letters; or irregular sizes, shapes, or slanting of letters
- Has unfinished words or letters or omits words
- Experiences inconsistent spacing between words and letters
- Exhibits strange wrist, body, or paper position
- Has difficulty previsualizing letter formation
- Copying or writing is slow or labored
- Shows poor spatial planning on paper
- Has cramped or unusual grip; may complain of having a sore hand
- Has great difficulty thinking and writing at the same time when taking notes or during creative writing

Strategies

- Suggest the use of a computer
- Avoid chastising students for sloppy and careless work
- Give oral exams
- Allow the use of a tape recorder during lectures
- Allow the aid of a note taker
- Provide note outlines to reduce the amount of writing required
- Reduce coping aspects of work, for example, by provided preprinted math problems
- Allow the use of wide-rule paper and graph paper
- Suggest student's use pencil grips and/or specially designed writing aids
- Provide two alternatives to written assignments, such as videotaped or audiotaped reports

Dyscalculia

Dyscalculia affects a person's ability to understand numbers and learn math facts. Individuals with this type of learning disability can also have poor comprehension of math symbols, struggle with memorizing and organizing numbers, have difficulty telling time, or have trouble with counting. (Disabilities, Types of Learning Disabilities n.d., Cortiella and Horowitz 2014)

Signs and Symptoms

- Has difficulty with counting, learning number facts, and doing math calculations
- Had issues with measurement, telling time, counting money, and estimating number quantities
- Has trouble with mental math and problem-solving strategies
- Shows difficulty understanding place-value concepts, quantities, number lines, positive and negative values, and carrying and borrowing
- Has difficulty understanding and doing word problems
- Has issues with sequencing information or events
- Exhibits difficulty using steps involved in math operations
- Has issues understanding fractions
- Is challenged when making change and handling money
- Displays difficulty recognizing patterns with adding, subtracting, multiplying, or dividing
- Has issues communicating math processes
- Has issues understanding concepts related to time, such as days, weeks, months, seasons, quarters, etc.
- Exhibits difficulty in organizing problems on the page, keep numbers lined up, and following through on long division problems

Strategies

- Allow the use of figures and scratch paper
- Use diagrams and draw math concepts
- Provide peer assistance
- Suggest the use the graph paper
- Suggest the use of colored pencil to differentiate problems
- Work with manipulatives
- Draw pictures or word problems
- Use mnemonic devices to learn the steps of a math concept
- Use rhythm in music to teach math facts and set steps to a beat
- Schedule computer time for drill and practice for the student

Associated Deficits and Disorders

While not designated as specific subtypes of LD, several areas of information processing are associated with LD. Weaknesses in the abilities to receive, process, associate, retrieve, and express information can often help explain why a person has trouble with learning and their performance. The inability to process information efficiently can lead to frustration, low self-esteem, and social withdrawal. Understanding how these areas of weakness impact individuals with LD and ADHD can be beneficial in planning for effective instruction and support (Horowitz, Rawe and Whittaker 2017). Let's look at these areas.

Auditory Processing Disorder (ADP)

Auditory Processing Disorder (APD), also known as Auditory Processing Deficit, is a weakness in the ability to understand and use auditory information. APD adversely affects how sound, which travels unimpeded through the ear, is processed and interpreted by the brain. Also known as Central Auditory Processing Disorder, individuals with APD don't recognize the subtle differences between sounds in words, even when these sounds are loud and clear. They can also find it difficult to tell where sounds are coming from, to make sense of the order of sounds, or to block out competing background noises. (Auditory Processing Disorder n.d.)

Signs and Symptoms

- Has trouble with auditory discrimination (i.e., the ability to notice, compare, and distinguish the distinct and separate sounds in words—a skill vital for reading)
- Has trouble with auditory figure-ground discrimination (i.e., the ability to pick out important sounds from a noisy background)
- Has issues with their auditory memory (i.e., short-term and long-term abilities to recall information presented orally)
- Exhibits issues with auditory sequencing (i.e., the ability to understand and recall the order of sounds and words)
- Has issues with spelling, reading, and written expression
- Has difficulty processing and remembering language-related tasks but may have no trouble interpreting or recalling nonverbal environmental sounds, music, etc.
- May process thoughts and ideas slowly and have difficulty explaining them

29

- Misspells and mispronounces similar sounding words or omits syllables; confuses similar sounding words (e.g., celery/salary; belt/built; three/free; jab/job; bash/batch)
- May be confused by figurative language (i.e., metaphors, similes) or misunderstands puns and jokes; interprets words too literally
- Is often distracted by background sounds/noises
- Finds it difficult to stay focused on or remember a verbal presentation or lecture
- May misinterpret or have difficulty remembering oral directions and difficulty following a series of directions
- Has issues comprehending complex sentence structure or rapid speech
- "Ignores" people, especially if they're engrossed in something
- Asks "What?" a lot, even when has heard much of what was said

Strategies

- Use visual cues, signals, handouts, and/or manipulatives to supplement with more intact senses
- Reduce or space out given directions and give cues such as asking, "Ready?"
- Reword or help decipher confusing oral and/or written directions
- Teach abstract vocabulary, word roots, and synonyms/antonyms
- Vary the pitch and tone of your voice, altering your pace and stressing keywords
- Ask specific questions as you teach to find out if students do understand what you're teaching
- Allow students five to six seconds to respond (i.e., "thinking time")
- Have students constantly verbalize concepts, vocabulary words, rules, etc.

Visual Processing Deficit

Visual Processing Deficit, also known as Visual Processing Disorder, is a weakness in the ability to understand and use visual information. (Cortiella and Horowitz 2014)

Signs and Symptoms

- Has issues with visual discrimination (i.e., the ability to notice and compare the features of different items and distinguish one item from another)

- Has trouble with visual figure-ground discrimination (i.e., the ability to distinguish a shape or printed character from its background)
- Experiences issues with visual sequencing (i.e., the ability to see and distinguish the order of symbols, words, or images)
- Exhibits issues with visual motor processing (i.e., using visual feedback to coordinate body movement)
- Has trouble with visual memory (i.e., the ability to engage in short-term and long-term recall of visual information)
- Experiences issues with visual closure (i.e., the ability to know what an object is when only parts of it are visible)
- Has problems with spatial relationships (i.e., the ability to understand how objects are positioned in space)

Nonverbal Learning Disabilities

Nonverbal Learning Disabilities describes the characteristics of individuals who have unique learning and behavioral profiles that can overlap with Dyslexia, Dyscalculia, and Dysgraphia but differ in significant ways. Most notably, these individuals often have strengths in the areas of verbal expression, vocabulary, reading, comprehension, auditory memory, and attention to detail. (Non-Verbal Learning Disabilities n.d., Cortiella and Horowitz 2014)

Signs and Symptoms

- Experiences issues in math computation and problem-solving
- Has trouble with visual-spatial tasks and motor coordination
- Has problems reading body language and with social cues and seeing the "big picture" in social and academic contexts

Executive Functioning Deficits

Executive Functioning Deficits is like the CEO of the brain. It's in charge of making sure things get done from the planning stages of the job to the final deadline. Executive functioning issues aren't considered a disability on their own. They're weaknesses in a key set of mental skills. And they often appear in kids with learning and attention issues. (Parent Guide 2015) EFD describes weaknesses in an individual's ability to plan, organize, strategize, remember details, and manage time and space efficiently. These are hallmark characteristics in individuals with Attention-Deficit/Hyperactivity Disorder (ADHD) and are often seen in those with LD.

Signs and Symptoms (Lambek, Tannock and Dalsgaardall 2011)

- Finds it hard to figure out how to get started on a task
- Can focus on small details or the overall picture, but not both at the same time
- Has trouble figuring out how much time a task requires
- Does things either quickly and messily or slowly and incompletely
- Finds it hard to incorporate feedback into work or an activity
- Sticks with a plan, even when it's clear that the plan isn't working
- Has trouble paying attention and is easily distracted
- Loses a train of thought when interrupted
- Needs to be told the directions many times
- Has trouble making decisions
- Has a tough time switching gears from one activity to another
- Doesn't always have the words to explain something in details
- Needs help processing what something feels/sounds/looks like
- Isn't able to think about or do more than one thing at a time
- Remembers information better using cues, abbreviations or acronyms

Treatment for Learning Disorders

New neuroscience research is deepening our understanding of the differences in brain structure and function in children with learning and attention issues. Brain scans and other tools are also helping researchers measure the biological impact that instructional interventions have on children who learn differently, including those with dyslexia, ADHD and other issues. (Horowitz, Rawe and Whittaker 2017)

Learning disabilities and ADHD are lifelong, but treatable. The signs of learning disabilities and ADHD can be evident from a young age. The Mayo Clinic reports "some children are naturally slower learners and might need time to develop reading, writing and math skills. Others, however, have disorders that affect their ability to learn." The American Academy of Child & Adolescent Psychiatry states "learning disorders are caused by a difficulty with the nervous system that affects receiving, processing, or communicating information. They may also run in families." (Learning Disorders No. 16 2013)

According to The State of LD: Identifying Struggling Students article, "without enough support, however, children with unidentified disabilities may not reach their full potential and risk falling behind and having to repeat a grade. This could lead to other problems, including dislike of school, absenteeism and dropping out." Many other researers agree that students who repeat a grade may eventually be identified with a learning disability after they have fallen far behind whereas others may leave school without ever having been identified.

The debate continues regarding the clear issue of why students are still struggling in school.

Researchers have cited the following factors as to why student's learning challenges go unnoticed: over identification of minority students, underrepresentation of the school's total population, parents not wanting their child to be labeled, learning issues are misinterpreted or overlooked by teachers, or interventions are not working for students. If nothing is done to identify and help remediate a child's learning disorder in the classroom, long term consequences will impact family and workplace relationships, too.

Learning disorders aren't the same as mental or physical disabilities, and don't reflect a child's intelligence. Instead, learning disorders affect a child's ability to complete a task or use certain skills, particularly in school. Mayo Clinic adds three other factors that might influence the development of learning disorders include: (Learning disorders: Know the signs, how to help 2016)

- **Genetics.** Some learning disorders, such as reading and math disorders, are hereditary.
- **Medical conditions.** Poor growth in the uterus (severe intrauterine growth restriction), exposure to alcohol or drugs before being born, and very-low birthweight are risk factors that have been linked with learning disorders. Head injuries might also play a role in the development of learning disorders.
- **Environmental exposure.** Exposure to high levels of lead has been linked to an increased risk of learning disorders.

Mayo Clinic suggests five ways that learning disorders can be treated. They are extra help, individualized education program (IEP), therapy, medication, and complementary and alternative medicine. (Learning disorders: Know the signs, how to help 2016). Parents, school administrators, teachers, and children do not have to despair. There is hope for students struggling with a learning disorder or learning disability. This next section focuses on appropriate methods to assist schools and parents with solutions to deal with a student's learning gaps.

Learning Disabilities

An LD cannot be cured or fixed. However, with the appropriate support and intervention, people with LD can achieve success in school, at work, in relationships, and in their community. However, "there's a higher reported incidence of learning disabilities among people living in poverty, perhaps due to the increased risk of exposure to poor nutrition and environmental toxins (e.g., lead, tobacco, and alcohol), along with other risk factors during their early and critical stages of development". (Horowitz, Rawe and Whittaker 2017)

Working with struggling students seem simple in description, but is complicated in its approach and implementation of effective instruction in the traditional public schools and perhaps non-existent in the private schools. Parents are demanding more for their children in the areas of timely identification and for effective classroom instruction. Thanks to the push by parents of children with learning disabilities, legislation continues to be at the forefront of ensuring these children will be guaranteed a free and appropriate education (FAPE). New studies and laws have surfaced that addresses turning research into education practices.

Interdisciplinary research, funded by the *Eunice Kennedy Shriver* National Institute of Child Health and Human Development and the Institute of Educational Science, is making progress in defining, differentiating, and treating specific learning disabilities. "Research confirms that SLDs are plural. Using a single criterion for identifying SLD is not supported by research." (Wolf and Berninger 2015)

Research, laws and outcries from the parent work hand-in-hand to ensure students learn and master basic reading skills up to third grade so that from that point on they read to learn. The academic performance for students with learning disabilities is bleak. According to the 2014 State of Learning Disabilities: Facts, Trends and Emerging Issues, the academic performance and school outcomes are as follows:

- **One-third** of students with LD have been held back (retained) in a grade at least once.
- **One in every two students** with LD faced a school disciplinary action such as suspension or expulsion in 2011. (Only students served in the category of emotional disturbance received more disciplinary actions.)
- Students with disabilities—including those with LD—are much more likely to be retained in grades than their peers who don't have disabilities.
- School outcomes for students with disabilities vary significantly across racial and ethnic demographics. While there are no LD-specific data about these students, overall data about this population indicate that:

○ Black students with disabilities are almost three times more likely to experience out-of-school suspension or expulsion than white students with disabilities and twice as likely to experience in-school suspension or expulsion. (Cortiella and Horowitz 2014)

Early intervention is key to helping a child stay on grade level and not losing their motivation or healthy self-esteem for and about learning. In addition, frequent monitoring and intensive interventions are needed to determine if special education is warranted. According to the National Institute of Health (NIH), "the most common treatment for learning disabilities is special education." (Learning Disabilities Information Page n.d.) In states such as Texas, most students diagnosed as dyslexic may not qualify for special education instead they will receive reading support under a 504 plan.

Dyslexia

The third grade year is a pivotal year for students. This is when students have learned to read and now read to learn. Children who don't read well in third grade are four times more likely to leave school without a regular diploma compared to proficient readers. (Hernandez 2011) States are making third grade reading proficiency a top priority. In fact, by the end of 2016, 38 states passed laws to ensure that students have the foundational reading skills needed to enter fourth grade, when the focus of the curriculum changes significantly. Third-grade reading laws are leading many states to expand the use of early assessment, which provides professionals with tools to better understand and respond when a child is struggling to learn. (The State of LD: Understanding Learning and Attention Issues 2018)

Expanding early identification of reading challenges can help schools identify and address learning and attention issues before students fall far behind. Most third-grade reading laws provide for frequent monitoring and intensive interventions to help students reach reading proficiency standards. In 2016, former President Barack Obama signed into law, the Research Excellence and Advancements for Dyslexia Act (READ Act) requires the National Science Foundation (NSF) to spend at least $5 million per year on SLD research. Half of this funding must focus specifically on dyslexia. The law is aimed at producing new research that may lead to: identifying dyslexia earlier, training educators to better understand and instruct students with SLD or dyslexia, curriculum and educational tools for children with SLD and dyslexia, and implementing and scaling successful models of dyslexia intervention. (The State of LD: Understanding Learning and Attention Issues 2018)

Researchers maintain that best practice guidelines for early childhood education assert the value of using data to guide instructional practice in general. The kindergarten assessments help identify particular skills with which a student may be struggling, such as numeracy or literacy skills. Some states have jumped on the bandwagon for the kindergarten assessments. California, New York, and Iowa are using early assessments for children ages 3-5. Schools implement kindergarten entry assessments on the assumption that having more information about students when they enter school will facilitate improved student outcomes. In theory if educators gather diagnostic information about each student's strengths and needs, they can use it to differentiate instruction and thereby improve student outcomes. Likewise, early identification of learning difficulties allows schools to connect students with needed services. (Shields, Cook and Greller 2016)

The early entry assessments are especially helpful in identifying students who may need further testing for learning disorders such as dyslexia. The aim of early or entry assessments gives teachers and parents an opportunity to understand what a student knows and can do. The state dyslexia laws aim to improve early intervention and identification. States implementing laws share four components: specific definition of dyslexia aligning with their state's education code, universal screening in certain grades to find children who struggle with certain literacy skills, evidence-based interventions in instruction for students who have been identified as displaying signs of dyslexia, and professional development for teachers to learn how to identify and address dyslexia. (The State of LD: Understanding Learning and Attention Issues 2018)

For most of the reading and math disorders, specially trained educators can perform a diagnostic educational evaluation assessing a child's academic and intellectual potential and their academic performance level. Once this evaluation is complete, the necessary approach is to teach them learning skills by building on the child's abilities and strengths while correcting and compensating for their disabilities and weaknesses. Also, speech and language therapists may be involved.

Public schools are required to provide free and appropriate public education for kids with disabilities a Free and Appropriate Public Education (FAPE). (Laws & Guidance Civil Rights: Disability Discrimination 2012) But they aren't required to provide the very best services available. A child may have needs that are a little more broad than what might be offered at their school. So purchasing additional services could make sense for a parent. Or, if you feel more comfortable with a specific private therapist and want to maintain that relationship, that's also an understandable reason for going outside of school services. Here are some forms of therapy you might consider if you're searching for private options: (Goode 2018)

- Cognitive behavioral therapy
- Occupational therapy
- Social skills counselor
- Educational or language therapy/special needs tutor
- Speech therapy

Executive Functioning Deficits

Executive planning is often one of the criteria for disorders like ADHD and autism. But experts haven't decided how executive dysfunction should be defined on its own. It's not a recognized category in the Diagnostic and Statistical Manual (DSM). Psychologists can administer tests for executive functioning. They can give specific recommendations on how to help your child if the tests reveal an area of weakness. Understanding your child's difficulties is a group effort. The next steps in understanding your child's suspected condition includes the following: (Parent Guide 2015)

Diagnosis: Get a medical exam. See a specialist such as a licensed clinical social worker, educational diagnostician or child psychologist who will administer Questionnaires or screening forms, Intelligence testing and A child observation and interview. Then put all the information together to look at the results.

Treatment: Several kinds of professionals can offer strategies and support to both you and your child. Speech therapists, occupational therapists, psychologists, and reading specialists can all help with executive functioning issues. For example, cognitive behavioral therapy can provide your child with mental tools to start self-monitoring thoughts and behavior.

Unlike LD, features of this disorder can be attributed to neurochemical imbalances that can be effectively treated with a combination of behavioral, and, as needed, pharmacological therapies. Although ADHD isn't considered a learning disability, research indicates that 30 to 50 percent of children with ADHD also have a specific learning disability, and that the two conditions can interact to make learning extremely challenging for them. (Attention-Deficit/Hyperactivity Disorder (ADHD) 2018)

In summary, we have 13 categories for disabilities Under the Federal Law, IDEA (Individuals with Disabilities Education Act), These are the 13 categories of Special Education and one of them is Other Health Impairment

(OHI). Attention Deficit Hyperactive Disorder (ADHD), is getting much attention because it is one of the fasting growing brain disorder that falls under OHI. Unlike LD, features of this disorder can be attributed to neurochemical imbalances that can be effectively treated with a combination of behavioral, and, as needed, pharmacological therapies. ADHD isn't considered a learning disability, research indicates that 30 to 50 percent of children with ADHD also have a specific learning disability, and that the two conditions can interact to make learning extremely challenging for them. Although ADHD isn't considered a learning disability, research indicates that 30 to 50 percent of children with ADHD also have a specific learning disability, and that the two conditions can interact to make learning extremely challenging for them. Attention Deficit/Hyperactivity Disorder (ADHD) 2018) I would be remiss if I didn't take the time to introduce you to ADHD and bring it to life for you. Because this disorder is often misunderstood and is getting so much attention, I decided to dedicate an entire chapter on it.

Chapter 4

Understanding ADHD

Attention-Deficit/Hyperactivity Disorder (ADHD)

Defining ADHD

Attention Deficit Hyperactive Disorder (ADHD) isn't a disorder of the modern age. It may have been first described in the medical literature in 1763 by Scottish physician Sir Arthur Crichton, who observed patients so unable to focus that "the barking of dogs, an ill-tuned organ, or the scolding of women, are sufficient to distract patients of this description to such a degree, as almost approaches to the nature of delirium." Those patients, he noted, referred to their own symptoms, including anger "bordering on insanity," as "the fidgets." (Foley 2018)

ADHD and other learning challenges are lifelong, but treatable. ADHD is a brain-based disorder. ADHD is divided into three subtypes—children just with attention problems, those with impulse control and hyperactivity issues, and a group with a combination of the two. (Foley 2018) It's estimated that as many as one-third of those with LD also have ADHD, and like learning disabilities, this disorder is linked both to heredity (genetics), as well as to brain structure and function. (Attention Deficit Hyperactivity Disorder (ADHD) n.d.)

ADHD is a condition that becomes apparent in some children during the preschool and early school years. It's hard for these children to control their behaviors and/or pay attention. The American Psychiatric Association states in the Diagnostic and Statistical Manual of Mental Disorders (DSM-5, 2013) that 5% of children have ADHD, which equals to approximately 2 million children the United States. (Diagnostic and Statistical Manual of Mental Disorders 2013). Meaning in a classroom with 24 to 30 children, it's likely that at least one has ADHD.

ADHD by the Numbers

According to a 2016 parent report from the Centers for Disease Control and Prevention (CDC) (Attention-Deficit/Hyperactivity Disorder (ADHD) 2018):

- Approximately 9.4% of children 2-17 years of age (6.1 million) had ever been diagnosed with ADHD with the ages of 12-17 accounting for 3.3 million children

- The percent of children 4-17 years of age ever diagnosed with ADHD had previously increased, from 7.8% in 2003 to 9.5% in 2007 and to 11.0% in 2011-12 with rates increasing among older teens as compared to younger children.

For more information about this data, visit https://www.cdc.gov/ncbddd/ adhd/data.html.

Ethnicity and Gender

In addition, research compares ADHD according to ethnicity and gender. The following data suggest: (Foley 2018, Pastor, et al. 2015)

- Among all age groups, prevalence of ever diagnosed ADHD was more than twice as high in boys (13.2 percent) as girls (5.6 percent) to be diagnosed with ADHD.
- Among those aged 6–17, prevalence was highest among non-Hispanic white children and lowest among Hispanic children.

Other Conditions Surrounding ADHD

ADHD isn't considered to be a learning disability. It can be determined to be a disability under the Individual with Disabilities Education Act (IDEA), enabling a student to be eligible to receive special education services. ADHD, however, falls under the category of "Other Health Impaired" and not "Specific Learning Disabilities." Researchers found that ADHD exist with co-illnesses. Let's look at the data on the co-illnesses. (Pastor, et al. 2015)

- Nearly 2 of 3 children with current ADHD had at least one other mental, emotional, or behavioral disorder.
- About 1 out of 2 children with ADHD had a behavior or conduct problem.
- About 1 out of 3 children with ADHD had anxiety.
- Other conditions affecting children with ADHD: depression, autism spectrum disorder, and Tourette Syndrome.

Characteristics of Attention Deficit/Hyperactivity Disorder (ADHD)

The principal characteristics of ADHD are inattention, hyperactivity, and impulsivity. There are three subtypes of ADHD that are recognized by professionals: The predominantly hyperactive /impulsive type (doesn't show significant inattention), the predominantly inattentive type (doesn't show significant hyperactive-impulsive behavior sometimes called Attention Deficit Disorder (ADD), and the combined type (displays both inattentive and hyperactivity-impulsive symptoms). Children and adolescents with ADHD show difficulty focusing, being easily distracted, disorganization, and forgetfulness, which are not normal behaviors for their age.

The three types of ADHD, predominately inattention, predominately hyperactive-Impulsive, and combined type are explained below, along with their symptoms: (Evans, Owens and Bunford 2013)

ADHD Predominately Inattentive:

Children with this type of ADHD frequently display at least six of the following symptoms:

- Do not pay close attention to details or make careless mistakes
- Have difficulty paying attention
- Do not appear to listen
- Struggle with following instructions (or finishing tasks on time)
- Have difficulty getting organized (or managing time)
- Avoid or dislike tasks that require a lot of thought
- Lose things
- Are easily distracted
- Are forgetful in daily activities

ADHD Predominately Hyperactive-Impulsive:

Children with this type of ADHD frequently display at least six of the following symptoms:

- Fidget with hands or feet
- Have difficulty staying seated
- Run about or climb excessively
- Have difficulty working or playing quietly
- Act "motorized"– (being restless and have trouble being still)
- Talk a lot
- Blurt out answers to questions or finish other people's sentences
- Have difficulty waiting or taking turns
- Interrupt or intrude upon others

ADHD Combined:

- These children are hyperactive and have trouble paying attention. They frequently show at least six symptoms from both of the lists above.
- To be diagnosed with ADHD, children must show some symptoms before they are 12 years old. They also must have difficulties in at least two settings, such as at home and at school.

Treatment for Attention Issues

Oftentimes, educators are frustrated when it comes to managing students with behaviors such as hyperactivity and impulsivity. Some teachers and administrators strongly believe ADD can also stand for A Deficit in Discipline, where corporate punishment is needed instead of medication.

For a clearer picture on ADHD behaviors, here's is a letter written by one of my former kindergarten teachers concerning a parent that was initially in denial until she was held accountable by the teacher, principal, and myself.

Zuri's Story-ADHD Bares Down on Behavior

Zuri is a 5-year old student that was placed in my class mid-September 2002. Zuri's a beautiful African-American child with a bright smile and a big heart. When Zuri entered my class, my colleagues said that she might need some medication for attention issues. I didn't meet Zuri's mother, Ms. Banks, until the parent-teacher conference in October. Ms. Banks appeared to be in denial about her daughter's emotional stage and stated that the doctor didn't feel that medication was necessary. I informed Ms. Banks about Zuri's behavior in class. Whenever Zuri cannot have her way, she begins to cry, kick chairs, and fall on the floor. I must place Zuri in a time-out at least three to four times a day. Ms. Banks stated the reason for Zuri's behavior is that she had spoiled her daughter. I informed her that Zuri must follow class rules and exhibit self-control. Each time I shared with Ms. Banks Zuri's progress in class, she appeared upset that Zuri was having difficulty. Ms. Banks is very protective of Zuri. Therefore, I had to be selective with my words when explaining Zuri's day.

One Friday afternoon, Ms. Banks approached me in front of the gym and asked how Zuri was doing in class. I informed her that Zuri was having difficulty with testing. She became distraught and stated that

Zuri didn't have these problems at her old school and that it only started once Zuri started attending in my class. Zuri's mom asked for her daughter's removal from my class. Since this upset Zuri's mom, I told Ms. Banks that I needed to take my class into the gym. Ms. Bank came inside and approached me again. While standing there, I noticed a backpack on Ms. Banks' shoulder. I attempted to remove Zuri's classwork to review it with her mother. Ms. Banks jerked the backpack away from me and angrily said, "This is not her backpack." I felt it was best if I walked away from Ms. Banks to avoid a scene in front of the children. Ms. Banks followed me to the other side of the gym floor. My principal heard Ms. Banks and called us into an office. While in the office, Ms. Banks stated that her daughter did excellent classwork at her previous school. I suggested a conversation with her doctor again to explore the possibility of Zuri using a treatment plan such as medication. The principal set up a meeting for 3:30 p.m. the following Monday.

I worried about the incident all weekend. I have more 30 years of experience working with children and have never had a parent request the removal of their child from my class. At this point, I felt that I had a parent who was in denial and her child needed my love and support.

On the following Monday, we had the meeting, and Ms. Banks once again expressed her concerns about Zuri's behavior and academic progress. Ms. Banks was calm and began to admit the truth that Zuri didn't do well in her other school. She also stated that she would speak to her doctor about medication for Zuri. She apologized for the things she had said. Ms. Banks admitted that Zuri loves her teacher and wanted to remain in my class. My principal confirmed that she wouldn't remove Zuri from my class. However, Zuri would have to follow class rules, and if that were a problem, she would have to administer corporal punishment (paddling). I told Ms. Banks why I became a teacher and the love I have for my students. I stated that I would do anything for my students, but Zuri must follow school rules. Ms. Banks began to cry and said that she feels like she is a lousy mother. She informed us that she's also in school and cannot spend quality time with her children. Ms. Banks has made a tremendous change in support of Zuri's academics and discipline. Zuri now realizes that she will not be allowed to exhibit unacceptable behavior in class. I am blessed because I have 100-percent support from Ms. Bank and my principal. Mattie Ford—Kindergarten Teacher

Some researchers and medical professional strongly disagree that ADHD is not bad parenting nor children acting bad. ADHD is not about children eating too much sugar, lack of discipline and structure or eating the wrong foods.

Researchers at the National Institute of Mental Health (NIMH), National Institutes of Health (NIH), and across the country are studying the causes of ADHD. Current research suggests ADHD may be caused by interactions between genes and environmental or non-genetic factors. Like many other illnesses, a number of factors may contribute to ADHD such as genes; cigarette smoking, alcohol use, or drug use during pregnancy; exposure to environmental toxins, such as high levels of lead, at a young age; low birth weight; and brain injuries. (Attention-Deficit/Hyperactivity Disorder (ADHD): The Basics 2016)

"There are anywhere from 25 to 45 genes that are considered high-candidate genes for ADHD," says leading ADHD expert Russell Barkley, PhD, clinical professor of psychiatry, Virginia Treatment Center for Children and Virginia Commonwealth University Medical Center in Richmond, VA. "But there are several we're reliably sure of, and some of those are the genes related to dopamine regulation in the brain." There are dopamine receptors on certain neurons (nerve cells) to which dopamine delivers its various messages, such as pay attention, control yourself, feel good, and do that thing that made you feel good again, the latter reflecting its role in promoting both addiction and learning. Dopamine transporters also protrude from the neurons that produce dopamine. (Barkley, What Causes ADHD? 2017)

Barkley said a version of the DAT-1 gene that builds the dopamine transporters has a version of that gene that's longer than normal. It produces too many of the transporters and gobbles up the dopamine before it has a chance to bind to dopamine receptors. This dopamine related gene make neurons less receptive to dopamine's effects, he said. As a result, there is no dopamine and a child has difficulty learning, focusing, have low motivation, and can become depressed. The researcher added that "other genes recently linked to the disorder strengthen the idea that ADHD is a fundamental communication system gone awry, a short-circuiting of the transmission between cells." (Foley 2018, Barkley, What Causes ADHD? 2017)

ADHD Treatment

"Inattention and hyperactivity are highly and disproportionately prevalent among school-aged urban minority youth, have a negative impact on academic achievement through their effects on sensory perceptions, cognition, school connectedness, absenteeism, and dropping out, and effective practices are available for schools to address these problems," Dr. Charles E. Basch wrote in the Journal for School Health. "This prevalent and complex syndrome has very powerful effects on academic achievement and educational attainment, and should be a high priority in efforts to help close the achievement gap." (Basch 2011)

Research has shown that approximately 3 percent of the student population has ADHD, yet only 7 to 10 percent of this population might be taking medication to address its symptoms. Other Health Impairments (OHI) is just one of the 13 categories of Special Education. Even though the number of students is incomparable to the total LD students, this is the fastest growing category because of the ADHD population. (39th Annual Report to Congress 2017)

Staying on task or focused is very challenging for an ADHD individual despite having an average or high IQ. For example, some children have an imbalance of chemicals in the brain fails to grasp new concepts when being introduced and often keeps their peers from learning and their teachers from teaching. When a child distracts his or herself from learning because of ADHD or distracts other students from learning, it's a major problem that must be addressed immediately. Teachers must be adamant about the student getting some help so they can focus on teaching learning skills by building on an ADHD child's abilities and strengths while correcting and compensating for disabilities and weaknesses.

Intervention strategies for ADHD include controlling the symptoms of the social and behavior challenges combined with remediation of academic challenges. Understanding ADHD is the first step. The American Academy of Pediatrics suggests ADHD evaluations should be conducted for children ages 4 or older who demonstrate academic or behavioral challenges and show signs of inattention, impulsivity, or hyperactivity. (ADHD: Clinical Practice Guideline 2011)

Understanding Treatment Options

Early intervention is central to dealing with attention issues. "Early screening – as soon as pre-K or kindergarten – is critical for children," said E. Mark Mahone, a child neuropsychologist, research scientist and the director of the Department of Neuropsychology at the Kennedy Krieger Institute in Baltimore. He explains that without early intervention, coexisting – also referred to as "comorbid" – conditions may not be easily detected and therefore not properly treated. "An ADHD diagnosis typically occurs at age

7," Mahone says, noting that symptoms may have been present for several years prior. He says those are "critical years" in terms of a child's brain and social development. "If there's a delay between ADHD symptom onset and treatment, there's a missed opportunity to reduce comorbid assessments with this condition." (Reynolds 2017)

Once a child has been officially diagnosed by a medical doctor, then treatment options for ADHD should include:

- Behavior therapy, including training for parents
- Medications
- School accommodations and interventions

The 2011 clinical practice guidelines from the American Academy of Pediatrics (AAP) recommend that doctors prescribe behavior therapy as the first line of treatment for preschool-aged children (4–5 years of age) with ADHD. Parent training in behavior therapy has the most evidence of being effective, but teachers and early childhood caregivers can use behavior therapy in the classroom as well. (Research Confirms What Many Teachers Know: Learning Disabilities Are Plural 2015)

For children 6 years of age and older, AAP recommends both behavior therapy and medication as good options, preferably both together. For young children (under 6 years of age) with ADHD, behavior therapy is recommended as the first line of treatment, before medication is tried. Good treatment plans will include close monitoring of whether and how much the treatment helps the child's behavior, and making changes as needed along the way.

According to the Subcommittee on ADHD, Steering Committee on Quality Improvement and Management, behavioral treatments, psychostimulant medication, and their combination are the most widely studied and accepted treatments for attention deficit/hyperactivity disorder (ADHD). A number of studies, suggest that the most effective short-term treatment for ADHD appears to be a combination of pharmacologic and behavioral treatment. (ADHD: Clinical Practice Guideline 2011)

Behavior Therapy and Parent Training

Most children with ADHD have problems in daily life functioning in many areas including academic performance and behavior at school, relationships with peers and siblings, noncompliance with adult requests, and relationships with their parents. These problems are extremely important because they predict long-term outcome of children with ADHD. How a child with ADHD will do in adulthood is best predicted by three things— (1) whether his or her parents use effective parenting skills, (2) how he or she gets along with other children, and (3) his or her success in school. (Behavior Therapy for Children with ADHD: An Overview 2016)

Psychosocial treatments are non-medical, which focus on these problems rather than the core symptoms of the disorder, so they are effective in treating these important domains. Second, in contrast to medication, behavioral treatments teach skills to parents, teachers, and children with ADHD, and these skills help overcome their impairments and are useful for a child's lifetime. Because ADHD is a chronic condition, teaching skills that will be valuable across the lifetime is especially important. It is important to note that many psychotherapeutic treatments are *not* behavior modification. Thus, traditional individual therapy, in which a child spends time weekly with a therapist or school counselor talking about his or her problems or playing with dolls or toys, is not behavior modification.

Children with ADHD often show behaviors that can be very disruptive to others. Behavior therapy is a treatment option that can help reduce these behaviors. It is often helpful to start behavior therapy as soon as a diagnosis is made.

The goals of **behavior therapy** are to learn or strengthen positive behaviors and eliminate unwanted or problem behaviors. Behavior therapy can include behavior therapy training for parents, behavior therapy with children, or a combination. Teachers can also use behavior therapy to help reduce problem behaviors in the classroom. Other considerations of behavior therapy includes the following: (Behavior Therapy for Children with ADHD: An Overview 2016)

- In **parent training in behavior therapy**, parents learn new skills or strengthen their existing skills to teach and guide their children and to manage their behavior. Parent training in behavior therapy has been shown to strengthen the relationship between the parent and child, and to decrease children's negative or problem behaviors. Parent training in behavior therapy is also known as behavior management training for parents, parent behavior therapy, behavioral parent training, or just parent training.
- In **behavior therapy with children**, the therapist works with the child to learn new behaviors to replace behaviors that don't work or cause problems. The therapist may also help the child learn to express feelings in ways that do not create problems for the child or other people.

Psychologists, licensed counselors, and licensed social workers can provide behavior therapy. The American Academy of Pediatrics recommends behavior therapy at the following ages: (Behavior Therapy for Children with ADHD: An Overview 2016)

- Age 4-5 years: Behavior therapy first, before trying medication
- Age 6 -11 years: Behavior therapy and medication, preferably together
- Age 12–18 years: Medications, behavior therapy as treatment

Please note that behavior therapy training for parents is effective for managing disruptive behavior in young children through age 12. For school-age children, parent training and behavior therapy with children can be very effective when used in combination.

Understanding ADHD and Medication

Dr. Lara Honos-Webb contends that ADHD is a gift. In the book titled The Gift of ADHD, Honos-Webb revealed" the current understandings of the diagnosis as a disorder and review a countertrend in psychology that argues that differences are not disorders." The clinical psychologist said that a child's "spaciness, distractibility, and impulsiveness are essential attributes for promoting creativity." "Children with ADHD who have been labeled as spacy often have the capacity to solve problems created by rigid modes of thinking," Honos-Webb said. "Daydreaming is the fount of creativity in that it is essentially the process of engaging the imagination creates dreams of new and original possibilities not yet existing in the world." (Honos-Webb 2005)

While some researchers may not agree with the ADHD creativity or giftedness that is described by Honos-Webb, it is true that these children can go on to find their niche in the world. Those symptoms that drive parents and teachers crazy can be turned into creative geniuses as Albert Einstein, an inventor or Walt Disney who captivated millions of young children and adults alike with Disney cartoons and movies. Just for a few minutes or so, the co-author of this book bares the memories of growing up as a misunderstood child on planet all alone with no research or treatment plan. Here is a look at an ADHD confession by my wife, Yvette McClure.

ADHD Confession - Madness or Medicine?

There are many people who may read my story about adult ADHD and call it crazy, you're out of your mind, or whatever descriptive adjective you can imagine. At the end of the day, please remember I told you—ADHD is real! It gets worse into adulthood.

I recognized that my hormones were raging and acting strangely once I turned 49. I was having anxiety attacks, frequent visits to the emergency room and my husband was sick and tired of me being sick. The romance was rocky at best. I started to believe that maybe I was really sick and had some type of real medical issue.

It wasn't until my family doctor started questioning my behaviors at home and with social and work-related activities. This made me reflect on growing up in the 60s and 70s with a motor that just would not shut or slow down. I participated in the band's flag corps, Future Business Leaders of America, Spanish club, Sigma Gamma Rho Sorority Rhoer's Club for high school girls, promoted my own radio talk show, part of a singing group called the Shreveport Emotions, sewed everything I wore, and the list could go on and on. Academically, I could not stand school. I had a history of not doing well in school and underachieving. I felt inferior to my siblings who were on the honor roll and in the honor society. I graduated from high school with a low "C" average. I daydreamed in school my entire childhood and teen years. I took notes profusely and could remember every word. I just struggled comprehending because I zoned out when the teacher taught the lesson or I could not wait on the teacher to provide examples or practical application of the information. I was well-liked by my teachers who would pass me with a low grade.

I majored in journalism because I covered stories that enabled me to go to every event, be in the know about everything in college. This was my dream career and job. I was always curious about people, places and things. I made better grades in my major than the basic courses of math, science and even the fourth level of Spanish where they spoke no English. I could not concentrate when I read a book. By the grace of God, I graduated in four years with the help of summer school classes just to stay on track and balance those classes that were a struggle.

Life into adulthood became very frustrating. I suffered with chronic boredom. I had a low tolerance for frustration. I believed in getting the job done immediately and removing anything or anyone in my life that causes frustration. Everyone was too slow—talking, moving, making decision. I found it hard to listen to others in a conversation. In the workplace, I had trouble focusing on future projects or the past. I was focused on "right now" and "hurry up, let's go." I never couldn't organize paperwork on a job. I left it in piles on my desk. I knew exactly where every document was stacked, how it was written or typed especially with color and you better not bother it. It would take me forever to complete those boring tasks. My employer called it excuses and procrastination. I called it boredom. In a 10-year timespan, I changed jobs every 16-18 months.

I was hypercritical of myself. I always felt everyone else's job or life was so much better than mine. I felt I didn't look right, hair wasn't right, clothes weren't right, and I didn't wear the same outfit twice. I struggled with impulsivity. I saw those shoes, purse, or outfit—I had to have it. It would stay in my mind until I got it or I realized it was sold.

As a stay at home mom, my ADHD superpowers helped me to manage children and a husband. My husband was timely and believed in being early. Who does that I pondered? Although I am early bird with energy in high gear from 5 a.m.- 2 p.m., I was challenged by habitual lateness. I got up at 5 a.m. every morning just to get the children to school for 8 a.m. I lost track of time. I daydreamed and planned everything out in my mind. It only took me five minutes to apply make-up, but one hour to pick something out of my closet until finally I reorganized my clothes and shoes by color and style. In addition, I spent 15 minutes looking for my car keys and occasionally my cell phone.

We were entrepreneurs so I had the privilege of working in my home office as a Public relations and special events consultant. I could concentrate so intensely on an event or researching that I block out everything else. My hyperfocus trait became the story of my life. I would get so involved in the project that I would lose track of time. Hyperfocus means that you are not conscientious that the time is flying by. Because I was so absorbed in a task, I became an expert at getting it done even more quickly. I would sometimes deviate from work and start shopping on line looking at hundreds and hundreds of pieces of clothing for an already packed closet. Time ran out. Time to pick up the kids and the work was undone. I often had the super energy to stay up all night or late with three or four hours of sleep to get the project finished.

My mind constantly was in over drive and forward motion. In fact, I drove fast everywhere I travelled. I hated driving more than one hour. I rather fly any day than drive out of town.

The older I got, the more I noticed the ADHD symptoms. I became principal of FOCUS Learning Academy, a school specializing in working with dyslexia and ADHD children. When I wrote the charter school application in 1997, I tried to ignore the signs and symptoms of the very children who would attend this school. In fact, I had so many of the challenges like those children that I became excited to work with them. I lived like those children growing up. We had no name for those signs, symptoms or characteristics.

At the charter school, I was on symptom overload. I carried laptop bag, a food bag, and another bag filled with papers. I had to have bags everywhere I go, at the airport, in the car, office, bedroom, kitchen table, etc. You name it. I believed that out of sight, out of mind. The school system consisted of too many meetings. I zoned out during those long meetings. In my new job, mood swings, fidgeting, anxiety, talking too much, and frustrations were mounting and becoming more prevalent. I could not get anything done at work but people issues all day long. I pushed papers at night. I found myself eating supersized bags of candy or nuts as a coping mechanism. Enough was enough!

All of these increased emotional symptoms and sicknesses led me to my doctor. After my doctor and I completed the rating scales protocol, the markings were so high that my doctor said "I was off the chart." He official diagnosed me with the combined type of ADHD. With counseling, it was determined that I would be prescribed Vyvanse medication. Every 90 days, I counsel with the doctor as well as take a urine test. Today, I manage ADHD with structure where I write down everything including a daily to do list. I put dates on my cell phone calendar with alerts to ensure timeliness with meetings or appointments, and set a time limit for projects. I have simplified everything in my life by developing a filing system and throwing away paper stacks, gave away half of my clothes and get an outfit out the night before to wear the next day, journal as a way to reflect on my daily actions, and able to sit through long meetings, and have better relationships with family and friends. *ADHD Confessions by Yvette McClure, co-author and wife of Leroy McClure, Jr.*

Formal Diagnosis

Medication was not my wife's first option for ADHD or it shouldn't be the first choice for a child with ADHD characteristics. Once a parent recognizes the struggles at home or a school exhaust all other accommodations and modifications, such as a structured environment, preferential seating, diet changes, and parental support, then a formal evaluation must be conducted to rule out health issues too.

In the case of Zuri's behavior, the teacher believed this was a result of lack of parent disciplining at the home. In my experience, there are two sides to a coin regarding how to treat students who exhibit ADHD characteristics. Some teachers believe that many students should be medicated while some parents believe that this medication isn't for the students, but should be given to teachers especially those who struggle with classroom management.

There is no single test to diagnose ADHD. The best way to find out whether your child has ADHD is to have him or her see a pediatrician, psychiatrist, psychologist, neurologist, or social worker familiar with ADHD. A visit with the doctor will help to diagnose the child and also determine if the child may have other conditions.

To make an ADHD diagnosis, the primary care clinician should determine that Diagnostic and Statistical Manual of Mental Disorders, Fifth Edition criteria have been met (including documentation of impairment in more than one major setting); information should be obtained primarily from reports from parents or guardians, teachers, and other school and mental health clinicians involved in the child's care. The primary care clinician should also rule out any alternative cause. (ADHD: Clinical Practice Guideline 2011)

Research indicates that medical treatment increases brain activity and gives a person with ADHD more "mental energy" to control their thoughts and actions. Taking ADHD medications are much like a near-sighted person using the aid of eyeglasses to help the person focus. No one should feel embarrassed about using ADHD medication. Taking this medication doesn't mean someone is too stupid or weak to control himself, just like wearing eyeglasses don't imply that someone is too slow or weak to control their eyesight.

Only medical doctors can prescribe medication for an ADHD child, not a teacher. The primary care clinician should prescribe Food and Drug Administration–approved medications for ADHD with the assent of the adolescent (quality of evidence A/strong recommendation) The evidence is particularly strong for stimulant medications and sufficient but less strong for atomoxetine, extended-release guanfacine, and extended-release clonidine (in that order) (quality of evidence A/strong recommendation). (ADHD: Clinical Practice Guideline 2011)

The most commonly used stimulant medications that "stimulate" (increase) certain activity in the body's central nervous system, including the production and activity of neurotransmitters. Most medications approved for the treatment of ADHD are stimulant medications. When taken as prescribed, they generally help improve the symptoms of ADHD by promoting alertness, awareness, and the ability to focus. (Glossary of Terms 2018) Stimulant medicines for ADHD are Vyvanse, Adderall, DextroStat, Dexedrine, Cylert, and Ritalin. Note, it's important to know what medicine can and cannot do.

Medication Warnings

According to the Children and Adults with Attention-Deficit/Hyperactivity Disorder (CHADD), the best-designed long-term treatment study—the Multimodal Treatment Study of Children with ADHD (MTA)—was conducted by the National Institute of Mental Health. The MTA studied 579 children with ADHD-combined type over a 14-month period. Each child received one of four possible treatments: medication management, behavioral treatment, a combination of the two, or the usual community care. The results of this landmark study were that children who were treated with medication alone, which was carefully managed and individually tailored and children who received both medication and behavioral treatment experienced the greatest improvements in their ADHD symptoms. (Psychosocial Treatment for Children & Adolescents with ADHD 2017)

Warnings about possible side effects of prescription medications are updated frequently. To stay abreast of recent warnings that may have been issued on your child's medication, visit the U.S. Food and Drug Administration Consumer Education/Information website, and ask your pharmacist for an update each time you refill the prescription. (Stuart 2014)

Hopefully, by understanding the symptoms and behaviors of learning or mental disorders, it may enable people to seek treatment and establish programs for those with these underlying issues.

ADHD medication can't be used to:

- Teach good behavior, reflective thinking, nor remove old behaviors

- Teach skills the child has missed, such as late school work or social skills, nor can it teach a child what to focus on
- Teach a child how to deal with feelings or learn how to control anger or deal with frustration, nor can it make a child happy
- Motivate the child to do something, such as trying new skills

ADHD medication can be used for the following:

- Decreases a child's activity level, so he or she can sit longer and run less
- Enables the child to focus longer, so he or she can accurately do more work
- Improves a child's attention and helps them to listen longer, which decreases their impulsivity; the child will follow the rules better and think before acting
- Decreases reactivity, so the child is less aggressive

ADHD at Home - Tips for Parents

Following are examples that might help with your child's behavior (Parent Guide 2015):

- **Create a routine.** Try to follow the same schedule every day, from wake-up time to bedtime.
- **Get organized.** Encourage your child to put schoolbags, clothing, and toys in the same place every day so your child will be less likely to lose them.
- **Manage distractions.** Turn off the TV, limit noise, and provide a clean workspace when your child is doing homework. Some children with ADHD learn well if they are moving, or listening to background music. Watch your child and see what works.
- **Limit choices.** Offer choices between a few things so that your child doesn't get overwhelmed and overstimulated. For example, offer choices between a few options, such as this outfit or that one, this meal or that one, or this toy or that one.
- **Be clear and specific when you talk with your child.** Let your child know you are listening by describing what you heard them say. Use clear, brief directions when they need to do something.
- **Help your child plan.** Break down complicated tasks into simpler, shorter steps. For long tasks, starting early and taking breaks may help limit stress.

- **Use goals and praise or other rewards.** Use a chart to list goals and track positive behaviors, then let your child know they have done well by telling your child or rewarding efforts in other ways. Be sure the goals are realistic—baby steps are important!
- **Discipline effectively.** Instead of yelling or spanking, use timeouts or removal of privileges as consequences for inappropriate behavior.
- **Create positive opportunities.** Children with ADHD may find certain situations stressful. Finding out and encouraging what your child does well — whether it's school, sports, art, music, or play — can help create positive experiences.
- **Provide a healthy lifestyle.** Nutritious food, lots of physical activity, and sufficient sleep are important; they can help keep ADHD symptoms from getting worse.

Understanding School Accommodations and Interventions`

While kids with ADHD can be gregarious, their impulsiveness can create problems, often alienating others, including siblings, teachers, and classmates. They don't wait their turn, interrupt others, are easily frustrated, take wild risks, and their emotions can spill over like water at a rolling boil: They may be hot-headed, lash out violently, or have temper tantrums. All of this carries enormous social cost in school and on the playground.

They're forgetful, tend to procrastinate, and are disorganized. They have a hard time putting in the time and effort to achieve a goal, particularly if it's something like finishing a school project on a topic that doesn't interest them. Some are chronically late.

Here are some tips to share with teachers for classroom success: (Barkley, Classroom Accommodations for Children with ADHD 2008)

- Make assignments clear – check with the student to see if they understood what they need to do
- Give positive reinforcement and attention to positive behavior
- Make sure assignments are not long and repetitive. Shorter assignments that provide a little challenge without being too hard are best.
- Allow time for movement and exercise
- Communicate with parents on a regular basis
- Use a homework folder to limit the number of things the child has to track
- Be sensitive to self-esteem issues

- Minimize distractions in the classroom
- Involve the school counselor or psychologist

School Programming and Supports

Behavior therapy programs coordinating efforts at school as well as home might enhance the effects. School programs can provide classroom adaptations, such as preferred seating, modified work assignments, and test modifications (to the location at which it is administered and time allotted for taking the test), as well as behavior plans as part of a 504 Rehabilitation Act Plan or special education Individualized Education Program (IEP) under the "other health impairment" designation as part of the Individuals with Disability Education Act (IDEA). It is helpful for clinicians to be aware of the eligibility criteria in their state and school district to advise families of their options. Youths documented to have ADHD can also get permission to take college-readiness tests in an untimed manner by following appropriate documentation guidelines. (ADHD: Clinical Practice Guideline 2011)

Instructional Interventions

The last place that an ADHD child wants to be is seated in a classroom all day long. Paying attention, writing assignments off of the board, or remembering what the teacher just said are a nightmare for some ADHD students. Teachers have to work triple time to manage the behavior and instruction for those students. The Children and Adults with Attention-Deficit/Hyperactivity Disorder (CHADD) has provided useful tips for teachers to help them optimize the learning environment for working with ADHD students. The instructional interventions are as follows (Tips for Educators 2016):

- **Introducing Lessons** - Students with ADHD learn best when structure is incorporated throughout lesson planning. Having a sequence that follows a basic routine and maintains a level of consistency are both vital.
- **Summarize the activities of the whole lesson visually and verbally**- what the student will learn and the activities you will use to teach it.
- **Present learning objectives in many ways**- write them on the board, say them aloud, ask students to repeat them, or ask students to copy them off of the board

- **Describe behavior expectations**- Tell students how they are expected to behave during the lesson.
- **List materials**- Be specific. Tell students the materials they will need during the lesson
- **Include time limits**- Tell students how long they will have to work on each activity, and consider setting a timer to help them externally see the time.
- **Teaching the Lesson**- presenting new material to students and letting them practice, connect it to prior knowledge, ample opportunities to practice the material with you guiding, with other students, and on their own. Provide feedback, different types of tools to help students who are struggling.
- **Stick to the plan**- sets expectations for the whole lesson. Follow the outline you have given, reinforce structure and consistency within a lesson. If changes are made, provide explanations so that they become predictable.
- **Review the previous lesson**- Since students have deficits with their working memory, help students recall previous knowledge by reviewing it. This practice will not only reinforce the previous lesson, but also help them remember the new lesson.
- **Provide guidance to stay focused**- Since ADHD student lose focus easily, they might become captured by a day dream or other activities in the classroom. During lessons, help them stay focused by using tools such as guided notes, colors, mnemonics, and probing questions.
- **Check for understanding**- ask open-ended questions, guide the class to the answer, allow students to answer collectively, and lastly answer on their own
- **Give students enough time**- more processing time is needed to learn new tasks. transfers responsibility from the teacher to student through four stages (I do, we do, you do together, you do alone).
- **Provide extra support**- Watch for students who are having difficulty comprehending the information. Provide extra help by explaining the material in a different way, using more examples, or having another student serve as a peer tutor.
- **Break work into small steps**- divide assignments into smaller pieces. break tasks into steps and keeps them engaged, setting them up to successfully complete an entire assignment.
- **Incorporate assistive technology**- participate actively and may help them organize their thoughts; on a computer or tablet or write on the board are ways to make assignments more engaging.

- **Provide time reminders and model how to pace-** need help managing their time, provide consistent and frequent reminders, model for students how to pace and work within a given time limit, stay on task and complete their work in the allotted time.
- **Ending a Lesson-** Conclude your lesson and help students transition to the next activity smoothly, finish strong so that you can transition to the next lesson
- **Summarize key points-** solidify the new knowledge they learned by reviewing the key concepts. Repetition is a must use open-ended questions to have students explain what they learned, or you can restate the objectives.

For more information on helpful tips for working with ADHD students, please visit www.chadd.org.

Professionals Who Can Help

There are many trained professionals who can help your child. Ask your child's teacher or a resource consultant for names of individuals who can help. Contact one of the organizations in LD Resources for additional suggestions and information. Here is the list of professionals who can help: (Parent Tips LD online LD Basics 2014)

- Audiologist – measures hearing ability and provides services for auditory training; offers advice on hearing aids.
- Educational Consultant – gives educational evaluations; familiar with school curriculum but may have a background in special education issues.
- Educational Therapist – develops and runs programs for learning and behavior problems.
- Learning Disabilities Specialist, Certified Academic Language Therapist or Licensed Dyslexia Therapist – a teacher with specific training and credentials to provide educational services to students with learning disabilities and their teachers.
- Neurologist – looks for possible damage to brain functions (medical doctor).
- Occupational Therapist – helps improve motor and sensory functions to increase the ability to perform daily tasks.
- Pediatrician – provides medical services to infants, children, and adolescents; trained in overall growth and development including motor, sensory, and behavioral development (medical doctor).

- Psychiatrist – diagnoses and treats severe behavioral and emotional problems and may prescribe medications (medical doctor).
- Psychologist (Clinical) – provides psychological and intellectual assessment and treatment for mental and emotional health.
- School/Educational Psychologist – gives and interprets psychological and educational tests; assists with behavior management; provides counseling; consults with parents, staff, and community agencies about educational issues.
- Speech and Language Therapist – helps children with language and speech difficulties.

Understanding Learning Styles

Researchers agree that all students learn differently. With that being said, have you ever wondered why you are bored or tuned out the teacher, your parent, a clergyman, a spouse, or anyone who is talking or teaching you something? Lay your worries aside. Many people give directions, explanations or any conversation the way they typically learn and understand. In a general conversation, this may work for the average person. However, in a formal setting, at least half of the participants or audience may have zoned out.

For instruction to be effective, educators must learn to teach children according to their learning styles. I use the biblical reference of Matthew 7:7 says, "Ask and it shall be given to you, seek and you shall find, knock and the door shall be open" (NIV 2011) to illustrate how people learn. The learning modalities consist of an auditory, visual, and kinesthetic way of learning.

Do you know your learning style or the learning style of your child or your students? If not, let's determine your learning style by a check mark or circle that describe you, your child, or a student accordingly. The area with the highest number of circles or check marks is your dominant learning style. Discuss the results with your child, student or perhaps an accountability partner.

Visual Learning Style

- Asks for verbal instructions to be repeated
- Watches speaker's facial expressions and body language
- Likes to take notes to review later
- Remembers best by writing things down several times or drawing pictures and diagrams

- Is a good speller
- Turns the radio or TV up really loud
- Gets lost with verbal directions
- Prefers information to be presented visually (i.e., on flipcharts or a chalkboard)
- Is skilled at making graphs, charts, and other visual displays
- Understands and follows directions on maps
- Feels the best way to remember something is to picture it in their head
- Follows written instructions better than oral ones
- Is good at solving jigsaw puzzles
- Gets the words to a song wrong
- Is good at the visual arts

Auditory Learning Style

- Follows oral directions better than written ones
- Would rather listen to a lecture than read the textbook's material
- Understands better when reading aloud
- Struggles to keep notebooks neat
- Prefers to listen to the radio than to read a newspaper
- Dislikes reading from a computer screen, especially when the background is fussy
- Frequently sings, hums, or whistles to themselves
- Can tell if sounds are the same or different when presented with two similar sounds
- Requires explanations of diagrams, graphs, or maps
- Enjoys talking to others
- Talks to self
- Uses musical jingles to learn things
- Would rather listen to music than view a piece of artwork
- Uses a finger as a pointer when reading
- Likes to tell jokes, stories, and makes verbal analogies to demonstrate a point

Tactile/Kinesthetic Learning Style

- Reaches out to touch things
- Collects things
- Talks fast using hands to communicate what they want to say

- Constantly fidgeting (e.g., tapping pen, playing with keys in pocket)
- Is good at sports
- Takes things apart and puts things together
- Prefers to stand while working
- Likes to have music in the background while working
- Enjoys working with their hands and making things
- Learns through movement and exploring the environment around them
- May be considered hyperactive
- Is good at finding their way around
- Is comfortable touching others as a show of friendship (e.g., hugging)
- Prefers to do things rather than watching a demonstration or reading about it in a book

Moving from Identification to Action

How many children in school with reading problems are we talking about? Although the public school does a poor job of identifying the students that need special services promptly, only 13 percent of them are documented. If there are 6.7 million students in special education, and over 2.3 million has been recorded as LD by the public district schools, then this number only represents one-third of the total number of LD students in public schools according to the Learning Disability Association (LDA). (The State of LD: Understanding Learning and Attention Issues 2018) In fact, there could be as many as 10 million children in the public district schools who are unable to read, and the majority of them remain unidentified. Educators are trying all types of programs to address the needs of these 2.3 million LD students who've been identified. My only concern is that educators use the right method to teach reading.

What's going on with the other 7.7 million unidentified children in the public district schools? They are falling through the cracks of our public school system, ending up as illiterate dropouts prison inmates. Research shows that 90 percent of prison inmates are former high-school dropouts. (Sainato 2017)

The major difference between the identified and unidentified LD students in public education is that the identified have an Individualized Educational Plan (IEP)that measures their academic progress. Although it's a legal document, if a child's academic progress cannot be measured, the IEP isn't working. For many years, too many LD students with IEPs graduated with a high school diploma and were unable to read it. This is a prime example of special education not working for an intelligent LD child.

Learning disabilities don't suddenly appear in third grade. Researchers have noted that the achievement gap between typical readers and those with dyslexia is evident as early as first grade. But many students struggle for years before they are identified with SLD and receive needed support, according to the National Center for Learning Disabilities. (Horowitz, Rawe and Whittaker 2017)

If an LD child is not identified by the third grade and adequately remediated, chances are he will receive social promotions throughout his school years and eventually develop learned behavior between the fourth and seventh grades. By then, he'll have no desire to learn, likely becoming an angry child with a behavior problem. The focus, then, is on his behavior and not on his reading problem. While this child once came to school daily ready to learn, he now arrives at school and keeps the teachers from teaching and his classmates from learning. Once enough behavioral documentation is in place, he likely will be sent to an alternative school. Unfortunately, there are a disproportionate number of African-American boys in these alternative school systems, which becomes the gateway to the penal system.

The alternative school system essentially becomes the recruiting ground for our prisons. How can you put hundreds of so-called bad boys together and expect a good or positive result? These students are considered as castaways and menaces to society. They are removed from mainstream classrooms and held in a holding tank until they perhaps age out of the system or drop out of school. Neither rehabilitation nor remediation takes place. Unfortunately, these students because of the products of negligent parents and educators. It should be a crime for a child to attend school every day and graduate 13 years later unable to read. Some adults should be placed in jail for gross negligence of adequately educating that child.

Chapter 5

Educational Disorder—
A Cancerous School System

"Each student is unique. While we cannot predict how any student will respond to an intervention, we can help students make progress and prevent struggles from becoming stumbling blocks. We can identify at-risk students early. We can use evidence-based instruction until the student becomes successful. And we can prepare teachers to work effectively with students who struggle with learning to read, write or do math. We must do each of these if we're going to identify problems as early as possible and make a difference for students. Too often we aren't doing enough early enough."—Louisa Moats, Ed.D., reading development expert and member of the International Dyslexia Association Council of Advisors (Moats and Farrell, Multisensory Structured Language Education.: Multisensory Teaching of Basic Language Skills 2005)

Undiagnosed and untreated learning disabilities in our school system are like cancer, a disease that continues to spread. Often, school administrators acknowledge that there's a problem. However, they ignore the problem, as if it will just go away. If they continue to wait for someone else to handle the problem correctly, this problem could fester and be just as deadly as cancer.

Unfortunately, in some cases, this cancer of learning disabilities has affected many lives due to educator procrastination. Why do educators feel this education crisis is an exception to their responsibility in intervening for our children?

Too many children in our public schools cannot read. According to the National Assessment of Educational Progress (NAEP), more than 50 percent of fourth-grade students aren't reading at their grade level. Also, chances of these students progressing to their appropriate grade level are slim to none. NAEP research data says, "as recently as 2013, only 14 percent of black boys and 18 percent of Hispanic boys scored proficient or above on the 4th grade reading component of NAEP compared to 42 percent of white boys and 21 percent of black and Hispanic girls." In fact, former President Barack Obama cites economic insecurity as one major issue affecting boys and young men of color disproportionately, said NAEP researchers. While

NAEP results don't provide a solution to closing the achievement gap, they do inform policymakers and educators as they work to improve the education of our nation's young Black males. (NAEP in the National Conversation: Black Male Achievement, n.d.)

If we don't timely identify the underachieving students, then properly and remediate them in addition to gaining support from their family, friends, staff, and community, these children will suffer due to this educational disorder. Our public schools must be proactive instead of being naïve or reactive in addressing illiteracy. Procrastination and miseducation will deeply hurt our children just like cancer if we do not treat this crisis with a state of urgency.

What Is a Cancerous Educational System?

According to *Merriam-Webster's Collegiate Dictionary*, a cancer is "a malignant tumor of potentially unlimited growth that expands locally by invasion and systemically by spreading to the other parts of the body." (Merriam-Webster.com n.d.) Malignancy produces poison, which deteriorates the body that results in death. My firsthand experience with cancer was with my sister, Deborah, who had stage 2 breast cancer. She was the second oldest of my four siblings and four years older than me. We were very close while growing up. She shaped my thinking about how quickly my family had to learn about the ugliness of breast cancer and how to not let it defeat her. Educational institutions must eradicate the cancerous growth of illiteracy or else our school systems could become diseased institutions.

When struggling readers invade our educational system, it's like the growth of a malignant tumor that can move into the lymph nodes. The entire school system has conditions that can manifest in the following ways:

- Increased student referrals for misbehavior
- A lack of specialized program funding
- Unqualified teachers
- Insensitive administrators
- The use of Ebonics
- Uninformed and ill-equipped parents and their lack of involvement
- The misperception of special education, including learning disabilities and ADHD
- An increase in high student dropout rate

Ignoring the condition of LD children becomes a direct correlation between illiteracy and crime. Academic struggles, which are left unreconciled, can produce the poison that slowly infiltrates the school system and can eventually result in school closure due to low performance. American schools will slowly fade away from their past successes into an unfortunate demise unless educators address those LD students appropriately and promptly.

Learning Challenges: A Cancerous Disease

Although cancer is a deadly disease that has killed millions of people across this country, it doesn't necessarily always mean death. Illiteracy must be addressed the same way doctors address cancers. Both diseases are urgent. The similarities in addressing cancer versus learning disabilities are early detection versus timely identification, proper diagnosis versus proper assessment, prognosis versus appropriate remediation, and support versus parental support. Let's take a closer look at the similarities between cancer versus a learning disability.

Early Detection vs. Timely Identification

If there's a cure for cancer, it's through early detection. The sooner you can detect cancer, the greater your chance is for survival. Research shows that breast cancer has four stages. During the first stage of growth, the chances for recovery is almost 100 percent. The second stage of breast cancer may require surgery or a lumpectomy. The third stage of growth means a radical mastectomy or double mastectomy to save the patient's life. The final and fourth stage is an aggressive level where it's possibly too late to save the patient's life, as their chances of survival are very slim to none. Being in denial of having cancer doesn't cause this disease to go away. Detecting it early, however, could enable the patient to seek the proper treatment and spare their life. They must disregard the saying, what you do not know won't hurt. In fact, it's quite the contrary—what you don't know due to a lack of early detection not only will hurt you, but it can kill you. Again, people will perish due to their lack of knowledge.

With cancer, *early detection* is paramount in determining the type, form, or severity of the disease. Diagnosing a student's academic challenges works the same way. Each cancer stage can represent a child's grade in school: *Stage 1—Kindergarten, Stage 2—1st grade, Stage 3—2nd grade, and Stage 4—3rd grade.* Look how many years of foundational learning has lapsed between a child's birth and when they're seven years old. No wonder minority students enter school two to three years behind their white counterparts, according to research. What is a timely manner for determining the type, form, or severity of a struggling reader? No catch-up plan is available for a struggling reader.

Research finds that any student having difficulty reading can be identified as early on as kindergarten and certainly by the third grade. Research further indicates that students who don't read proficiently by the third grade are four times more likely to exit the school system without a diploma than proficient readers. It is notable in breaking down the likelihood of graduation by different reading skill levels and poverty experiences. (Hernandez 2011)

Hernandez also notes that third grade is a pivotal point. "We teach reading for the first three grades and then after that children are not so much learning to read but using their reading skills to learn other topics. In that sense, if you haven't succeeded by third grade it is more difficult to remediate than it would have been if you started before then," Hernandez said. "Simply put, a child learns to read from kindergarten to third grade. A child reads to learn from fourth grade and beyond."

One of the best practices offered through FOCUS Centre of Learning included following a three-step plan to help children who were falling behind in reading or math in kindergarten through third grade. The steps are as follows:

1. The parent and the administrator must be notified immediately of the child's failure.
2. Teachers must provide supporting documentation, such as parent communication logs, a record of student interventions, and a performance action plan.
3. Administrator/teacher meetings must take place to monitor and review the child's progress.

Also, researchers recommend that progress monitoring should be conducted every six to eight weeks to determine if the remediation is successful.

If a child is lagging in academic growth between kindergarten and third grades, chances are this child will always remain behind unless intensive remediation occurs promptly. These first three years are pivotal because most children come to school with the desire to learn. They are very excited about school until learning becomes so laborious ultimately deflating their excitement. When this happens, you now must deal with a learned behavior instead of dealing with the real issue of camouflaging the situation. These children should not be placed in the corner or outside in the hallway, nor should they be sent to the principal's office because their teachers decided to focus on the learned behavior and not the real issue. Teachers must look at the amount of wasted time in educating these children when they are distracted by student behavior. Disruptive behavior can be a child's way of deflecting from his/her learning deficiency. Remember, students come to school every day to learn, not to ensure a teacher has a bad day.

Proper Diagnosis vs. Proper Assessment

With the early detection of a cancerous cell, proper diagnosis is essential. If there is a tumor, you must determine if it's malignant or benign. If it's benign, it means the growth is noncancerous. If the tumor is malignant, however, it is cancerous. The worst thing a doctor can do with a tumor is to open and aspirate it several times over several weeks or months without proper diagnosing it to see if the tumor is benign or malignant. In this case, timely identification is in order.

Like a child's reading problem, a suspected cancer patient undergoes a series of test to identify the *proper diagnosis*. After timely identifying a child with reading or learning difficulties, *properly assessment* is the next order of business before the doctor proposes a treatment plan. A proper assessment will help the child receive a proper course of action, ensuring that the appropriate therapy addresses their specific reading challenge. It's a necessary first step in closing the reading gap for a child.

The right battery of instruments determines if a child has a learning disability or any other challenge that's keeping him or her from learning. Educators must be proactive in obtaining the proper assessment for a child who's experiencing learning challenges before the third grade. This assessment must be given in the best interest of the child and not just for the exemption of a high-stakes state standardized achievement test. Remediation is aimless when you don't have a diagnosis. Many children fall through the cracks because their teachers focus on exempting them from their state's high-stakes accountability test, instead of properly assessing them for appropriate remediation. No reason exists for a child not to be evaluated or tested in first or second grade if their learning challenges are apparent and continue. In this case, the teacher needs to know as soon as possible the results of the battery of assessment, to implement the proper remediation and accommodations. During the first three years, teaches teach a child to read, and afterwards, a child reads on his or her own. Teachers must be certain that all students are reading at their grade level by the third grade or children with such difficulties will continue to lag and fall farther behind, possibly even dropping out of school.

Prognosis vs. Appropriate Remediation

The treatment for malignant breast cancer is normally a very comprehensive approach. Timing affects the treatment plan for cancer. Early detection can require as little medication or a lumpectomy with or without chemotherapy. Detection of malignant breast cancer in the last stage possibly may need a radical mastectomy, chemotherapy, and radiation. Unfortunately, there are many side effects from these treatments, such as loss of energy, loss of hair, low self-esteem, and ongoing nausea. Even though the side effects can be overbearing at times and a patient's recovery appears to be getting worse, their oncologist made the right *prognosis* to develop a treatment plan.

Like a prognosis, Dictionary.com defines remediation as "the action of remedying something". In this case, it's the giving of remedial teaching or therapy—the first of developing a treatment plan for a learning disability. For reading struggles, specialized programs must be suitable or proper for waging war to ensure a child learns to read. Appropriate remediation is like the prognosis or treatment of the breast cancer patient—their treatment plan is prescriptive and individualized.

I believe reading is the gateway to everything. Appropriate remediation for a child with a diagnosed reading disorder should be specific and personalized for him or her to read at grade level. Research shows that the majority of the students who're failing is due to reading difficulty. People no longer have shackles around their feet, they have them on the minds of our children who believe they cannot learn to read.

Social reformer, abolitionist, orator, writer, and statesman, Frederick Douglass said, "Once you learn to read, you will be forever free." (Shapley 2017) In 2016, on a trip to Washington, D.C., with 39 seniors from Triple A Academy, the sister school of FOCUS Learning Academy, I toured the house of Douglass. I was captivated by his extensive library filled with hundreds of books. I watched the amazement on the faces of six learning disabled students. Their eyes lit up when they heard the story of Douglass' fight to help African-American children learn to read.

I witnessed firsthand those same seniors in their therapy sessions at the FOCUS Centre of Learning and the charter school, FOCUS Learning Academy. Five of those six students had a reading problem, and they had an individualized educational plan specifically with remediation in a robust multisensory program. Through daily instruction in FOCUS' alphabetic phonics program, they learned phonemic awareness, phonics, fluency, vocabulary, and text comprehension. Their regular program was structured, sequential, cumulative, repetitive, and multisensory.

During their daily instruction, our teachers focused on each student's different learning styles. Research says most African Americans are auditory learners, which explains why African-American children can hear rap music, then recite it better than their ABCs (Garger 2001). Unfortunately, such a negative spin has been synonymous with the African-American race that if you put rap lyrics in a book, they likely would never read it.

Through the prescribed lessons associated with an alphabetic phonics reading program, teachers must be very objective when periodically measuring an LD child's academic growth. Success within this program translates into an increase in a child's improved self-esteem. It's ineffable when you see the metaphoric lightbulb lighting up when a child experiences excitement when learning to read fluently and comprehend a text's meaning. When a child tastes success, he will inform some people just like he will let them know about the ridiculing by others.

I firmly believe that accommodations and modifications without the appropriate remediation are a violation, not an acceleration, of that child's civil rights. Under no circumstances should a student walk across a graduation stage to receive a high school diploma and not be able to read it.

Support vs. Parental Support

Many patients with malignant breast cancer in the second, third, or fourth stages feel devastated and think they are going to die. They view cancer synonymous with death, and it doesn't help when their hair is falling out, and they're sensitive to odor, sounds, light, and food. In fact, during treatment, cancer patients despise all of this. What they need more than anything is support from someone who survived the disease. There is no better person to support, comfort, and offer hope to someone with the same trials and challenges. The patient's doctor, spouse, family, and a cancer survivor can come together forming a good strong support team for a cancer patient. Ultimately, this TEAM—Together Everyone Achieves More—can become a key to survival.

This type of team approach is also relevant to a child diagnosed with a learning disability, ADHD, or other learning disorders. It can also become a time-out for the teacher or parent to play the blame game. Research has determined that dyslexia is hereditary. The focus, however, must not be on who's to blame, but rather on how and who can help a child learn how to read. All parties involved need support. First, everyone must share in the responsibility of being equipped with as much information to assist the child in-school classwork and after-school homework. A team approach is imperative between the parent, teacher, and school administrator. They must establish a partnership as soon as possible so that the child will not continue to struggle in school and to keep the adults from pitting against each other. On many occasions, I've witnessed a child reach third grade and beyond and then began to misbehave to camouflage their academic struggles. He or she exhibits manipulative behavior, such as blaming the teacher when speaking to the parent and holding the teacher hostage by what the parent may or may not have said. If you're not careful, it may indeed become a tangled web instead of a much-needed team approach.

The biggest disguise in this game of charades is that the child continues to fall behind in school and his/her chances of graduating from high school decreases. During this time, parents and teachers want to live what even wise Solomon says in the book of Proverbs 17:28: "Even fools are thought wise if they keep silent." (NIV 2011) The team must work together for solutions so that they will avoid conflict with the parent and school.

Lawrence W. Lezotte, in his book titled *Learning for All*, clearly recognized that the struggle between the parent and teacher relationship can be contentious. Lezotte said, "It is clear to both teachers and parents that the parent involvement issue is not that simple. Parents are often as perplexed as the teachers about the best way to inspire students to learn what the school teaches." He further states, "The best hope for effectively confronting the problem—and not each other—is to build enough trust and communication to realize that both teachers and parents have the same goal—an effective school and home for all children!" (Lezotte 1997) No matter the child's struggle, like the cancer patient, the support team must work together, so everyone achieves more, especially the child.

In summary, learning disorders (LD) are not written on the forehead of our students; therefore, it is not easily discovered by parents, teachers and administrators. Despite the fact that new learning is more challenging for LD students and they have had many opportunities to learn, they still don't get it. This alone should signal red flags to the educators and the parents that something is wrong despite the child being smart in other areas or exhibits above average IQ. Signs and symptoms of LD students are prevalent, we must be aware of them and then be proactive in meeting the needs of these students immediately. Meeting the student's academic needs is not about passing the state standardized exam for that child to be successful, it is about the LD child being successful in life with prescriptive remediation and then being an asset, not a liability to our community.

Chapter 6
Centered Around Learning

Focus on Children in United States (FOCUS)

In the early 1980s, my brother Sammy moved to the Dallas area where he began working with dyslexic children at a private school specializing in working with learning disabled children. Sammy was excited when he finally found out why he'd struggled in school. He told me that he was so much like the students he coached at this private school and that he'd been diagnosed by professionals while teaching his students. These professionals diagnosed him with both dyslexia and auditory processing deficiency disorder, both of which had gone undiagnosed and interfered with his childhood and teenage school days.

Finally, Sammy's learning challenges were identified. Watching him grow up in the 60s and 70s with an undiagnosed reading challenge, in addition to the new information about learning disabilities, became the reason for me to become trained to help such students. Although I was a successful computer programmer for Texas Instruments in Dallas, Texas, I left my profession and became a certified specialist in learning disabilities and reading skills. In 1993, I became the first African American-male Certified Academic Language Therapist (CALT).

For the next eight years, I worked at two different private schools for students who were learning disabled. While there, I noticed that no students of color attended these schools because they cost more than $15,000 a year to attend. I realized I couldn't stop there. Children aren't born with insight into words, nor does it develop naturally without instruction. Many African-American children aren't afforded opportunities to learn outside of formal teaching. They need classroom instruction that explicitly addresses the connections between letters and sounds, which can make all the difference between reading failure and success.

I had a clear vision— "I must focus on the children in the United States"— especially minority male students because I didn't want any student growing into adulthood with academic struggles like Sammy. In 1993, I incorporated the FOCUS Centre of Learning, Inc., and received a 501(c)(3) tax-exempt status from the Internal Revenue Service (IRS). I began to focus on providing services to LD students at private and public schools.

I relied on faith. I resigned from my full-time private school job and began seeking funding from foundations to open a center to work privately with students. With a $20,000 grant from a local foundation, I opened the doors to FOCUS Centre of Learning, Inc., a viable alternative to both traditional public and private schools. The Centre provided educational services to children with LD, such as dyslexia and ADHD.

The Centre's mission was to provide a positive educational environment that enhances self-esteem; welcomes unique learning styles and individual talents; and promotes academic success by incorporating a multisensory approach to reading instruction, all while fostering sensitivity to cultural attributes to ensure the optimal development of the whole individual. It sought to assist those who are at-risk of failure because they cannot read or have other learning problems that interfere with the normal learning process.

From the beginning, the number one priority of the Centre's program was to teach 2,000 students to read by the year 2000, thus giving more students an opportunity to enhance their scholastic performance. Rather than serving as a school itself, the learning center was designed to improve the performance of students at the schools they attend. It targeted children who couldn't afford private school tuition and those likely to fall behind in the public school system without specialized training. Many of these children were minority students.

Ultimately, the Centre provided a unique opportunity for the interaction of the family, school, and community in a cooperative effort. Perhaps the most significant benefit for the children attending the Centre's activities was the development of a high sense of accomplishment and self-esteem. These strengths profoundly affected all areas of the lives of the children and helped them deal with dyslexia and other learning disabilities and failure.

I worked with more than 100 private students from 1995 to 1996. The Centre specialized in various remedial programs, comprehensive individual assessments and treatment services, community outreach, and a teacher-training program for educators and other professionals.

After the formation of this nonprofit organization, I served as the only program instructor who tutored students out of their homes. One year later, the program moved to a facility located in Richardson, Texas, a suburb 10 minutes north of Dallas. A ribbon-cutting and grand opening ceremony was held on December 15, 1995, commemorating the opening of the Richardson site. In November 1996, FOCUS opened its second location in the southern sector of Dallas County. The Centre's mission accomplished the creation of in-school and after-school programs for individuals ranging from kindergarten through adulthood.

Centre Services-A Prescriptive Plan

Our program and services were ideally suited to address the symptoms and signs of learning disabilities and reading disabilities, understand the cultural motivations and student resistance, and ensure long-term participation for students involved in our programs. The Centre offered structured in-school and after-school support programs with a reading curriculum, academic therapy sessions, teacher training, and community outreach. The staple programs of the Centre were Academic Language Therapy, Alphabetic Phonics, Teacher Training Program, and Community Outreach. The next sections give an overview of each of the programs.

Academic Language Therapy

One program offered by the Centre was Academic Language Therapy. This program emphasized the FOCUS Phonics taught with a trained classroom teacher or through a tape series with trained specialists and other remedial programs.

Alphabetic Phonics (AP)/FOCUS Phonics Program

Our remedial program was named Alphabetic Phonics (AP)/FOCUS Phonics Program. The program's curriculum covered 85 percent of the English language, and students who completed the program's eight schedules could usually score adequately at their grade level or above on standardized tests.

FOCUS Phonics program started with the pioneering research of Dr. Samuel T. Orton, a neuropsychiatrist, and the educational and psychological insights of Anna Gillingham, an educator, and psychologist. (Bates 2013-2018) Known as the Orton-Gillingham techniques designed for teaching children lacking a talent for language became the basis of a pilot study from 1965 to 1975 at the language laboratory at Texas Scottish Rite Hospital for Children in Dallas, Texas, under the direction of the late Dr. Lucius Waites, a noted medical doctor and a member of FOCUS's Advisory Board. The hospital's interdisciplinary team incorporated multisensory teaching techniques and current findings in learning theories and discovery teaching into the Alphabetic Phonics (AP) curriculum.

The FOCUS Phonics Program helped a child reach his or her maximum potential through a multisensory, structured, sequential, and cumulative program in reading, spelling, and writing. Also, the program included the Alphabet Principle, which consists of knowing the names and sounds of the 26 letters of the alphabet and the ability to write the alphabet and not sing the ABC song. Dr. Louisa C. Moats, *How Spelling Supports Reading*, said that "half of all English words can be spelled accurately on the basis of sound-symbol correspondences alone, meaning that the letters used to spell these words predictably represent their sound patterns. Another 34 percent of English words would only have one error if they were spelled on the basis of sound-symbol correspondences alone. That means that the spelling of 84 percent of words is mostly predictable. Also, it was estimated that only four percent of English words were truly irregular." (Moats, How Spelling Supports Reading And Why It Is More Regular And Predictable Than You May Think 2006)

With our FOCUS Phonics program, students learned decoding, word-attack skills, and listening skills. It's important to note that written words are composed of letters of the alphabet, which are intentionally and conventionally related to segments of spoken words. Also, this program featured reading comprehension skills. The program presented pre-reading and early reading skills in exciting and carefully designed programs that focused on sound-symbol association and letter recognition. Instruction in the use of organization and comprehension strategies occurred for all ages.

The most important aspect of the FOCUS Phonics Program was meeting each child at his or her academic level. This program was for students beginning in kindergarten who had average or above-average intelligence. It can be used to teach all children to read no matter if they have moderate to severe dyslexia. If a child has severe learning disabilities, he or she needs a longer and more intensive remedial training program. Yes, these students likely do show some progress, however, it's likely is less than compared to the rest of the class. In such cases, the principal suggested to the parent recommendations for special education services with an individualized educational plan for those students exhibiting severe LD characteristics.

Texas Scottish Rites Dyslexia Training Tapes Series

Created by the language laboratory at Texas Scottish Rite Hospital for Children in Dallas, Texas, the Texas Scottish Rites Dyslexia Training Tapes Series were available to students in the Centre's off-site after-school programs. Our organization's employees administered this self-paced tape series in small group sessions at the after-school program.

Language Therapy Sessions

A Language Therapy session was built on a step-by-step approach using intensive phonics. Alphabetic Phonics program was taught in private or small-group instruction of no more than 8 to 10 students. The program was taught in a small classroom environment by a Certified Academic Language Therapist (CALT). The benefit to a live classroom therapy session was an actively involved therapist who could immediately assist a student. Also, the CALT was able to improve a child's organizational and thinking skills and self-esteem.

Students used their auditory, visual, and kinesthetic senses as they interacted in the one-hour therapy sessions. This language therapy consisted of phonics with ABCs, long- and short-vowel sounds, beginning sounds, blends, ending sounds, clusters, digraphs, combinations, trigraphs, affixes, basic sight words, word-attack skills, etc. These skills taught all children to read, not just the dyslexic or ADHD child.

The language therapy sessions took place three days a week (Mondays, Tuesdays, and Wednesdays) during regular school hours when the children were more alert, and they didn't miss out on any after-school extracurricular activities. This program was divided into eight schedules: I, IIA, IIB, IIC, IIIA, IIIB, IIIC, and IIID. For example, a student who lagged behind two grade levels could learn to read at their grade level once four schedules were completed in two and a half years. Furthermore, this same student could advance grade levels ahead if all eight of the schedules were completed.

1—Timely Identification

We believed early assessment with objective measures was important. First, the principal, teachers, and/or counselor were asked to recommend a pool of students considered to be at-risk of failure in reading or show symptoms of dyslexia or other learning disabilities. Once these students were identified, they were properly assessed through the FOCUS Phonics Benchmark.

2—Proper Assessment Tools

A trained CALT conducted a pre-assessment called the FOCUS Phonics Benchmark on the identified students. FOCUS' assessment instrument determined a student's skill levels in the following four areas: the alphabet, handwriting, spelling, and reading. This assessment tool made our student diagnosis and program evaluation possible. This tool not only enabled a teacher to modify their teaching to meet a child's current proficiency level, but it also directed them forward.

3—The Implementation

All students who were assessed and diagnosed as nonreaders began an intensive one-hour academic language therapy session given three days a week during the hours designated by each campus' principal.

Each one-hour phonics session included 11 different multisensory activities that lead to skill mastery. The 2- to 10-minute activities took into consideration the short attention span of many students. The daily schedule is shown here.

Daily Schedule of Activities

Language

- Aspects of the development of language-Students were taught they can read, write, and spell 84 percent of standard English if they learned the code on which it was based (Moats, How Spelling Supports Reading And Why It Is More Regular And Predictable Than You May Think 2006).

Alphabet

- Alphabet study and practice leading to dictionary skills

Reading Decks

- Reinforcement activity to identify and instantly name each grapheme and translate it into speech sounds

Instant Deck

- Reinforcement activity to translate each speech sound immediately into the spelling letter that most often represents it

Multisensory Introduction of a New Letter

- Introduction of letters and letter clusters for reading, writing, and spelling through eight multisensory linkages

Reading Practice

- Application of the code for accuracy, fluency, and comprehension

Handwriting Practice

- Practice of cursive writing - emphasis on naming the letter before writing it

Spelling

- Support of the student's application of sound-symbol relationships learned by practicing the Instant Spelling Deck

Verbal

- Encouragement of organized oral expression; development of word pictures and expression transition to written expression

Review

- A brief review of the day's new discoveries and previously taught concepts

Listening

- Reading by the teacher of high-interest selections increased listening and comprehension skills, as well as providing a daily treat

The FOCUS Benchmark Assessment

Progress monitoring was essential to the effectiveness of the curriculum by monitoring the child's reading/language progress to provide practical strategies. A Language Therapy session begins with the FOCUS Benchmark Assessment, which was an informal assessment to determine a child's academic reading level.

The Centre used a modified version of benchmark measures that the Texas Scottish Rite Hospital staff developed, which were administered at intervals throughout each child's training to periodically determine their amount of growth in learning since the last measurement. This assessment tool contained a flexible non-standardized procedure for assessing the language comprehension. It measured the child's level based on where they were within one of the eight schedules of lessons within the AP curriculum, measuring their progress in reading and reading comprehension. Although this tool didn't conform to a national standardized test, it could be modified and used as a national assessment for all children.

The Centre's lead CALT worked with the program manager or supervisor to help ensure the success of each child based on his or her academic level as well as attendance. The language sessions emphasized mandatory attendance as part of its accountability review process. For a child to show significant progress, a minimum of 75 percent attendance was required. Written and signed commitments from their parents were also required for each participating child, which positively affected attendance.

Other Therapy Programs

Another program offered by the Centre was Speech Therapy Program. This program was designed to address various speech and language disorders, including neurological speech or language impairments, articulation, phonology, stuttering, voice disorders, hearing impairment and deafness, developmental disability, and difficulty in word retrieval. The Centre offered other computerized programs, such as Fast ForWord™, a revolutionary, computerized CD-ROM–based speech-language training program for children with language-learning impairments. This computer training was based on 20 years of research by two neuroscience experts named Dr. Michael Merzenich, from the University of California at San Francisco, and Dr. Paula Tallal, from Rutgers University.

This program taught rapid acoustic-processing skills and speech and language skills, including phonics, morphology, syntax, and grammar. The program benefited children ages 5 to 12 who had speech-language disorders and experienced difficulties in receptive phonology, listening comprehension, and age-appropriate general language ability. Training was eight weeks long with a one hour and 40-minute session given five times weekly in the child's home, at school, or at the Centre.

Diagnostic Testing and Treatment Services

The Centre provided diagnostic testing and treatment combined with a full battery of academic and psychological testing. We offered treatment services with a full-scale battery of tests for evaluation and assessment of intelligent quotient scores. Testing and evaluations were conducted only by appointment. The Centre's services included holistic assessment, intervention, consultation, and training services for students and families that enabled expedient identification and the appropriate intervention for every student.

Consultation sessions were held with teachers, students, parents, and or therapists to strategize a program specifically designed to address each child's individual needs, which also included pre- and post-consultations to measure their respective results. Our trained professionals assisted by attending ARD meetings and through the development of a child's individualized educational plan.

Community Outreach Programs

The Centre was on the cutting-edge of creating an enormous awareness campaign for individuals with different learning styles by offering effective solutions for their success in school and in life. The Centre believed that early diagnosis, appropriate intervention, and ongoing support were vital for LD children. Without such identification and intervention, learning disabilities can lead to severe consequences for the individual and for society, including loss of self-esteem, and consequently, dropping out of school, juvenile delinquency, illiteracy, and other critical problems. Research says that the majority of students who can't read by third grade will either drop out of school or end up incarcerated.

To combat this, the Centre began an extensive community outreach effort where we partnered with other professionals to provide the following to some public and private schools on a paid and pro-bono basis:

- Comprehensive reading instruction
- Extensive training in learning disabilities and specialized learning approaches
- Numerous diagnostic services

This outreach included workshops and seminars for students, parents, teachers, administrators, and other professionals.

Teacher Training and Consultation Services

> Learning is not attained by chance,
> it must be sought for with
> ardor and attended to with diligence.
> Abigail Adams, letter to John Quincy Adams, May 8, 1780
> **(Abigail Adams Quotes II: American First Lady**
> **(1744-1818) 2018)**

In 1997, more than 400,000 Texas public-school students took the Texas standardized reading test. (Snapshot '97: 1996-97 School District Profiles 1997) Recognizing the importance of the early development of reading skills necessary to succeed in school, the Centre researched how to reach more children in the Dallas area. Research has shown that with the additional training and expertise required to teach LD students and at-risk youth, many public-school systems seek to accomplish those goals by hiring outside consulting firms, further entailing other expenses. With the looming statistics on the correlation between illiteracy and crime, the compelling need for service delivery from the nonprofit sector is evident.

Historically, the prevailing notion about teaching has been that any teacher who uses effective teaching strategies should be able to teach any student. In terms of reading instruction, a plethora of research suggests that to improve student's reading skills, teachers must teach them to decode and comprehend various types of texts (McEwan, 2009; Shaywitz, 2005). However, the low reading test scores and widespread underachievement of many African-American students highlights the failure of this notion. Nationwide, countless teachers trained to use good teaching strategies continue to fail to meet the academic needs of many children with learning disabilities and students of color. The National Center for Learning Disabilities maintains that 70% of classroom teachers in elementary school say a significant challenge they face is lack of resources needed to provide instruction, related services and support to children with learning and attention issues. (The State of LD: Understanding Learning and Attention Issues 2018)

Over the last decade, research studies have overwhelmingly validated the AP (graphophonemic) approach to teaching reading as being fundamental to the success of all beginning readers, not only to those at-risk. The real issue is that teacher state certification programs don't focus on reading strategies nor interventions. Experts from the Texas Scottish Rite Hospital for Children state that "teachers report that cultural minority students and those learning English as a second language benefit especially from reading instruction which emphasizes the foundations of English and time-on-task activities to effect mastery."

Since 1995, the Centre has provided training to over 100 teachers who, in turn, have impacted thousands of children and families through advocacy, counseling, testing, and educational remediation services. The Centre trained teachers to work effectively with LD students in all types of educational settings.

Our Teacher Training Program's curriculum was based on the previously mentioned Orton-Gillingham theories and techniques. Dr. Orton personally initiated the clinical approach to the training and supervision of the academic therapist. This training program has been recognized as being effective for teaching basic language skills to all students, including those with dyslexia and related disorders. (Bates 2013-2018)

The FOCUS Teacher Training Program provided intensive preparation in the Alphabetic Phonics (AP) Reading Program, a multisensory structured system of teaching reading to learners who, for whatever reason, had failed to master that critical skill. Our 100-hour course included 70 classroom-instruction hours during the summer, 24 Saturday-session hours (four Saturdays during the school year), and five observations held during the school year.

Candidates attending the FOCUS Teacher Training Program were required to have a bachelor's degree for admittance. The program was an intensive two-year commitment that included 200 hours of classroom instruction, 820 teaching hours, and a minimum of eight demonstration observations. The program was taught by qualified instructors who are certified by the Academic Language Therapy Association (ALTA). Qualified instructors provided academic instruction, supervised demonstrations of teaching competency, and made on-site observations of those training to become a Certified Academic Language Therapist (CALTs). The FOCUS Centre of Learning was an accredited Academic Language Therapy Training Center.

Year One: The Year One Summer Session consisted of the Introductory Course, which was uniquely designed to teach classroom teachers a multisensory technique in a 70-hour introductory-level course with 21 hours of additionally required workshop attendance. Monthly follow-up sessions and observations were provided throughout the year to reinforce and support all aspects of the FOCUS Teacher Training Program. After completion of the first year's Introductory Course in classroom instruction, candidates were prepared to begin teaching situations—groups no larger than six students or one-to-one teaching situations. The final hours of training included a practicum component where each trainee was required to have 20 hours of therapy sessions with a student who experienced reading difficulty.

Year Two: During Year Two's Summer Session, the Advanced Course was held with demonstrations and participation required in curriculum workshops, which included four annual observations of each teacher using the techniques presented in the FOCUS AP class and seven workshops. Throughout the two-year training, specific reading, handwriting, written assignments, and competency checks were required. All training and teaching situations were conducted by qualified instructors (master teachers). Upon completion of the two-year program including the student contact hours and observations, teachers received a certificate of completion from the FOCUS Centre of Learning, Inc. with the title of Academic Language Therapist. Upon completion of the comprehensive examination by the Academic Language

Therapy Association (ALTA) with a passing score, teachers then received the title of Certified Academic Language Therapist (CALT).

Program Expansion: Our Teacher Training Pilot Program in Public Schools

This is the value of the teacher, who looks at a face and says there's something behind that and I want to reach that person, I want to influence that person, I want to encourage that person, I want to enrich, I want to call out that person who is behind that face, behind that color, behind that language, behind that tradition, behind that culture. I believe you can do it. I know what was done for me.— Maya Angelou (Tucker and Stronge 2005)

Although regularly trained classroom teachers may want to help a child who suffers from dyslexia and learning disabilities and/or those who are considered at-risk of failure because they cannot read, teachers don't always know how to instruct these students. Most regular-classroom teachers haven't been taught the appropriate methods of dealing with LD and at-risk youth by teacher-training colleges and universities.

With a growing incidence of learning disabilities occurring among the nation's children, the ability of schools to keep producing better results for all students will depend on better teaching. Unfortunately, many teachers haven't been adequately trained in strategies to help students with these disabilities. Due to budgetary constraints, private nor public schools have the additional funding needed to offer specialized LD programs specifically for training teachers in specialized programs. As a result, the Centre's CALT became a resource to regular classroom teachers and assisted them with specialized methods and techniques to teach their LD children.

In fact, principals from several Dallas Independent School District (DISD) elementary schools exhibited their support to our program by allowing teachers from their respective elementary school to learn our specialized multisensory techniques designed to work with at-risk.

In 1997, FOCUS partnered with DISD's District 5 and other supporters to provide a two-year comprehensive program to train 30 elementary teachers to work with at-risk children with learning disabilities such as dyslexia, ADHD, or a reading disability. The participating elementary schools from District 5 were Budd, Bushman, Ervin, Johnston, Lisbon, McMillan, Marshall, Miller, Mills, Oliver, Russell, Sequin, Starks, and Young.

Participation in the program by teachers improved the chances for all their students to meet Texas's goal: By the year 2001, 90 percent of the children enrolled in the third grade would achieve grade-level proficiency in reading in their language of instruction, and children would be able to pass the state's standardized test.

Dallas 75216 Initiative

In 1996, the Centre was awarded a grant from the State of Texas to provide a program of outreach services to 185 youth and parents in Dallas 75216 zip code, which has the highest crime rate in Dallas County. The program's goal was to alleviate family and community conditions that lead to juvenile crime, which was part of a comprehensive approach in supporting families and enhancing positive youth development. This initiative was a community-wide approach to promote strong bonds of family, school, and the community, thanks to the vision and direction of Texan Democratic State Senator Royce West. The project focused on education and gang-intervention programs.

During the 1996–1997 academic school year, the Centre implemented a structured and sequential program designed to teach reading and reading comprehension in three Dallas ISD elementary schools: Lisbon, Whitney Young, and Roger Q. Mills. We worked with 70 students in 75216, teaching them how to read through the FOCUS Multisensory Alphabetic Phonics (FMAP) Program. Through this program, the Centre discovered that some of the students were on their grade level according to their age, but they had little or no understanding of letters or words; therefore, they couldn't spell their name or birth month, and most tragically they couldn't read.

FMAP was designed to increase learning in one or more of the following areas: the alphabet, handwriting, spelling, and reading. Special attention was given to each youth, utilizing the multisensory AP technique, which enables a child to develop personal discipline and a sense of responsibility and to hone their cognitive abilities. The lessons were designed to help with timing, attention, concentration, creative problem-solving, and sequencing.

At the three elementary schools, the Centre gathered data and information about its effectiveness. Our findings showed the following positive results:

- The commitment of each school's principal and staff,
- The identification of youth who couldn't read,
- The use of an appropriate assessment device called a Benchmark Assessment that made both student diagnosis and program evaluation possible, and

- The discovery of public school teachers who wanted to become CALTs.

In addition, the FMAP program was implemented with the following:

Attendance— Because this program was very structured, sequential, and accumulative, near perfect attendance was mandatory. Consequently, a child's progress was also observed in self-esteem, positive attitude, and self-confidence.

Benchmark Assessments— Before the program began in September 1997, a trained Academic Language Therapist conducted a pretest assessment known as the Benchmark. This instrument determined the skill level in four areas: the alphabet, handwriting, spelling, and reading. All students assessed were diagnosed as nonreaders.

Class Schedule— Class schedules were determined as one hour per day, three days a week, for a nine-month period. Two classes were conducted from 9 a.m. to 10 a.m. and 10 a.m. to 11 a.m.

Curriculum— The AP program was divided into eight schedules: I, IIA, IIB, IIC, IIIA, IIIB, IIIC, and IIID. A child would be able to master 85 percent of the English language when they completed the eight schedules in two and a half years.

Student Selection— Students who were nonreaders were selected for the language therapy-based training. The first class consisted of second and third graders, while the second class consisted of third and fourth graders.

Trained Therapist— A trained CALT was assigned to the private- or public-school program. The CALT provided daily in-school language therapy to help accommodate each child's learning style.

An Overview of the FMAP Program at Public and Private Schools

In 1996, two African-American female teachers became the Centre's first CALTs. They were so inspired that they begged me to write a proposal to the private school they were employed to implement a one-hour reading program. Armed with another grant, I implemented an Orton-Gillingham–based AP program at Dr. Tony Evan's private school named Fellowship Christian Academy (FCA) in Dallas, Texas. I worked with two different groups of 10 students five days a week at FCA. Also, the other CALTs also provided a daily class for more students to ensure that more students would learn to read through the AP Program.

With a plea from the two African-American female CALTs, private-school parents witnessed the impact and gains made by their children in the private therapy sessions. However, the parents were also at a crossroad—a financial hardship of paying for tuition and for after-school private therapy sessions. It became a tug of war for the students we served because they needed help in-school as well as after. Their parents wanted both, but understandably private-school tuition won out over our after-school help.

The advantages of working with students in an in-school program include the following:

- Language therapy takes place during regular school hours when the child is more alert.
- The child doesn't miss after-school extracurricular activities.
- Instruction can be coordinated with current in-class assignments.
- There's no additional expense for the school.
- Assessed students are able to receive specialized training in a small group setting with a 1 to 10 teacher-student ratio.

Our Public-School Findings

At Lisbon Elementary, the first class consisted of second and third graders, while the second class consisted of third and fourth graders. Five of the twenty-three students transferred to other schools or classes before the year ended. Our classes were scheduled to meet three times per week; however, intensive preparation for the Texas Assessment of Academic Skills (TAAS) test occasionally interrupted the schedule. Before May, all students were assessed again using the Benchmark to determine their progress. It was confirmed that both classes had several students with strong symptoms of dyslexia and ADHD.

The most important aspect of the FMAP program was that we met each child at his or her academic level. Initially, our findings were alarming. Nineteen of the twenty-three students didn't know there were 26 letters in the alphabet, and none of the students knew that the letters of the alphabet consisted of vowels and consonants. However, after taking part in our FMAP program, all students showed significant progress in one or more areas in the basic concepts of reading.

Our findings revealed that the amount of a student's progress was directly related to his or her attendance. Data from the DISD reported a higher percentage of student absences in minority communities than in any other

Dallas communities. It was challenging to master our structured, sequential, and accumulative program with high absenteeism. However, the therapist recognized the importance of encouraging students by telling them to "make every day count" by attending school so they would have a higher chance of learning to read.

Through the FMAP program, new material was introduced daily. In most language therapy sessions, we started with learning and identifying the alphabet. When students mastered these skills in the Lisbon classes, they were excited and confident about moving on to the next level. Once several successes were experienced, most students continued to build on the foundation that had been established in a positive environment. Unfortunately, in the public schools, several students between the first and fourth grade continued to face failure each year because the foundation was never mastered. Therefore, illiteracy rates continued to rise because these students entered school far behind.

Our Private School Findings

Unlike Lisbon, FCA was a private Christian school where parents had to pay tuition. At this school, the Centre worked with 11 students for 18 months. We began our first class in January 1996 with students in a session from 1 p.m. to 2 p.m., three times per week. The class consisted of second- through fifth-grade students. The Benchmark indicated that most students were pre-Schedule I because all of them were assessed as nonreaders.

Unlike Lisbon, FCA students attended school more frequently due to their parent's financial obligation, and those who left the program did so because they left the school due to monetary issues. Six of the eleven students transferred to other schools by the end of the 1995–1996 school year. The next school year, the class began with five students, and all exhibited remarkable progress as they moved through Schedule I. During May 1997, all the students were reassessed with the Benchmark to determine their placement and development. Only those students who continued the program showed the most progress.

Our findings show that 8 of the 11 students didn't know that there were 26 letters in the alphabet. More than one-half of the students didn't know that the letters consisted of vowels and consonants. However, after taking part in our AP program, all students exhibited progress.

Moving Forward with FMAP

Students who acquire and apply the Alphabetic Principle early in their reading careers reap long-term benefits (Stanovich 1986) One of our four components to help a child read was *timely identification*. Research data clearly shows that reading skills are best developed at an early age. Suitable systematic development activities for young students must be available for students in grades first through sixth. We mustn't wait until children reach the third grade to teach them how to read. At least one-half of the African-American children aren't taught the alphabet before first grade. We believe the education received in childhood is the foundation upon which all later skills and abilities are built. It starts in the first grade or earlier.

For the 1997–1998 academic school year, we decided to continue with the same students from the prior year's program and expand the program to include a group of 10 first-graders. We used our Benchmark Assessment as a tool to monitor their reading/language behavior continuously to provide effective strategies, as well as conduct periodic reviews for accountability of what had been taught and what had been mastered.

Our FOCUS Program underwent an annual process (formative) and product (summative) evaluation. These two approaches were found to be the most effective for assessing program implementation and the quality of our service delivery. Additionally, research shows that the ability to carry out process and product evaluations can significantly assist in ensuring quality and cost-effective service delivery.

As this service delivery model became a staple in public and private institutions, we redesigned our evaluation tool to measure and report program progress in teacher recruitment, teacher training, the number of students impacted, and measurable improvement of student literacy levels.

The Sports Motor Program

With an emphasis on sports, we implemented a new Sports Motor Program. The goal of this program was to improve a student's perceptual motor-skill development, self-esteem, discipline, and attitude by focusing on personal growth and good sportsmanship and deemphasizing competition. Our sports program included the following:

- Weekend, summer, and year-round co-ed sports camps and basketball clinics
- Private or group lessons in basketball and motor-skill development

Sounding the Bell—More specialized learning!

My vision from God was clarified in the 1980s when I realized the tremendous toll that learning disabilities and poor reading skills had on my own family and the community-at-large. As I've mentioned, I felt compelled to advocate for these students because their learning problems stemmed from poor economic backgrounds, emotional issues, vision and hearing problems, or learning disabilities. The Centre's services cost money. As I spoke to parents and grandparents at various organizations and parent meetings, I realized that a high percentage of them lacked the financial resources for a private language therapy session not to mention no public transportation to the Centre's suburban location and their child could not attend one of the pilot school programs in inner-city Dallas.

In summary, students who can't read face an uphill battle in the classroom and in life. There are thousands of poor, inner-city African-American children battling dyslexia and other learning disabilities, as well. Without financial resources for extra after-school help or not living in the right attendance zone for a specific school, some of these students could possibly drop out of school or end up in prison. The Centre was challenged to do more than offer programs after school and at private schools and organization. It was time for the Centre's leaders to expand its vision. These children needed a tuition-free school specializing in research-based reading for challenge children like that offered by FOCUS Centre of Learning in the southern sector of Dallas where high crime and high academic failure existed.

Chapter 7

Charter Impact

Trestan's Story

Trestan Bills was a frustrated little boy. First grade was a disaster for him because the seven-year-old youngster was repeating it again. He entered school significantly behind his classmates in phonological awareness, knowledge of the alphabet, and vocabulary. He can't read. He has a reading disability.

Trestan was one of a sobering high number of public school children who have encountered reading difficulty. The personal and societal costs of these reading problems are enormous. Unfortunately, Trestan lived within an urban context where his basic physical, social/emotional, and psychological needs, along with his cognitive development needs weren't being met. In spite of his family's and teacher's ongoing concerns and high aspirations for his future success, they didn't demonstrate the living skills required to effectively broker available human service systems, nor the educational backgrounds necessary to fully support his cognitive and social development.

Trestan had an undiagnosed learning disability that required special education services in his school setting. However, before decisions could be made about the type of special education services provided, an evaluation was necessary by his school's psychologist. His public-school system had a two-year waiting list of assessments resulting from a lack of manpower.

Like Trestan, more than 50 percent of third-grade students studied were in danger of repeating the same grade due to having difficulty in reading and with spelling. All of them had something in common—an undiagnosed learning disability such as dyslexia or ADHD that required special education services in the school setting. However, before any decisions could be made about what special education services were needed, each child required a formal evaluation by a licensed school psychologist. However, these evaluations occurred one to two years later. When one of FOCUS' CALTs asked a student, "What are the two kinds of letters in the alphabet?", she replied, "ABCs and letters you mail at the post office."

The Centre targeted Trestan and other students from the four DISD schools located in the zip codes 75216 and 75224 in Dallas, Texas, communities with the highest crime rates in Dallas. The 1990 Census Report showed that unemployment, single-parent households, negative role models, drug and alcohol abuse, and teen pregnancy were all statistically high. Of these children, more than 52 percent of the third graders were reading below grade level. In these communities, 64 percent of these children were African American. Area elementary schools reported a daily average absentee rate of 14.5 percent or 105 children per day according to the Texas Education Agency's Public Education Information Management System (PEIMS).

Statistics showed that many adults in those zip codes experienced reading challenges as a result of learning disabilities or cognitive disabilities and didn't fare well in the mainstream society. These individuals were unemployed or underemployed and didn't possess the necessary skills needed for daily living or to help their children learn to read. However, this same group of adults was engaging in family life and charged with the responsibility of guiding a new generation of readers into the life of literacy that had alluded them. What we saw in those children was frightening. Research often says those students mirror the route taken by their parents, or if they're lucky, they end up living with grandparents who haven't the time, energy, or skills to ensure that the literacy process was taking place.

Due to a lack of parental support or understanding and/or financial resources, most African-American youth will not receive the necessary assessments to determine if their reading deficits are related to learning disabilities, or if they are at-risk of failure because they're low-readiness readers.

We realized it at the time that it was imperative to provide early intervention programs for children beginning in first grade. In doing so, we kept sounding the alarm that schools must give timely identification, proper assessment and evaluation, remediation and/or medication, and provide support to students who can't read. Those four components were necessary to intervene to prevent a child's retention in the same grade, being placed in a resource room, or eventually dropping out of school.

We implemented our program in those communities because they had the highest crime rate at the time in Dallas. There were clearly some socio-economic factors impacting the youth attending schools that were located in these communities. A large number of children lived with grandparents because their parents were either incarcerated or on drugs. Those students were profoundly influenced by radio and television. There was no encouragement to read. Frequently, there were no siblings or parents with post high school education. Those factors affected learning at their district home schools; therefore, the students were unable to learn the basic language skills of reading, writing, spelling, listening, and speaking clearly.

One Vision, One Mission

With the FOCUS Centre of Learning full operational, I realized it was time for the Centre to refocus its efforts to serve as a school itself, instead of a merely a one-hour program located in various schools or after-school youth support programs.

Our Centre posed a direct challenge to the local business community and government to provide monies to assess public school students who possibly were learning disabled. I received a postcard in the mail inviting our Centre to attend a meeting about charter schools, and my wife encouraged me to attend. It became clear that we should apply for a charter school. The Centre was a nonprofit organization that could easily rent a facility where we could offer our program to students in an all-day program. But starting a school to assist LD students meant we needed the support of the entire community of parents, churches, teachers, and administrators.

Before the advent of public open-enrollment charter schools, parents were required to send their public-schooled children to the school district in their residential area. Since their inception in 1995, charter schools gave parents the alternative educational option of another type of public school known as a charter school. These schools are required to meet state accreditation and accountability requirements. In some cases, they have operational flexibility in their type of curriculum, number of students, geographical boundaries, governance structure, etc. as well. Charter schools are sometimes referred to as schools of choice where parents can choose to send their children to a public charter school, rather than to their home- or default-school district.

After being inundated with many parental requests to provide a solution for the failing public schools in their surrounding communities, the FOCUS Centre of Learning, Inc., heard the cry. The Centre created the FOCUS Learning Academy, a charter school located in both Texas and Arkansas. These schools were designed to provide diagnostic, therapeutic, and educational services to children with learning disabilities and ADHD. The unique programs and services offered by FOCUS were for children with special learning needs with access to specialized education, diagnostic testing, language therapy, speech, and related services. The school's goals were to improve language skills, build confidence and hope, restore self-esteem, and provide students with positive learning experiences emphasizing the needs of the individual. The school also sought to increase the awareness of LD children and served as a significant community resource.

Once established, 75 percent of the students who attended the FOCUS Learning Academy were intelligent children with learning disabilities, and 25 percent were children who could adapt to learning in regular education classrooms. The school's curriculum was created to be in compliance with the essential requirements delineated in the Individuals with Disabilities Education Act (IDEA). It was also a model for special education delivery that was both a comprehensive reform model and moved the school toward a more innovative model of special education and related services.

Our curriculum was individualized, structured, and multisensory academic program with a model designed to challenge, stimulate, and adequately remediate the minds of students who'd had experienced difficulty in the traditional classroom. The school raised academic achievement through multisensory and success-oriented teaching techniques and small structured classes. We believed positive school experiences fostered the student's feelings of self-respect and competence essential for success in life.

Mission Accomplished: A Tale of Two Schools in Two States

FOCUS Learning Academy—Dallas, Texas

The charter school movement had just begun in Texas in 1996. To apply, I wrote a proposal to the Texas Education Agency. In September 1997, bolstered by a passion for students with learning difficulties and plagued by the failing Dallas public school system, the Centre's Board of Directors voted to create and apply for a charter school.

In November 1997, I drove the Centre's charter application on its due date to the Texas Education Agency located in Austin Texas. It had to be time-stamped by 5 p.m., but I got lost along the way, making it to the right office five minutes after closing time. I had missed the deadline. Emotionally, I was devastated. I cried and prayed. Yet, to no avail, our rejected proposal was mailed back to us.

In 1998, we decided to move our business from Dallas's northern suburbs to southern Dallas area to be closer to my consultant jobs in various public and private schools. At the time, my wife was seven months pregnant, very sickly, and trying to pack to move to our new home. Two months before the move, I received notice that the creation of the third generation of charter schools had begun and the agency was accepting applications. My wife cared for our son in her left arm as her right hand pecked away on the keyboard. We had to write our charter and turn it into the Texas Education Agency before the July 24th deadline.

Naturally, my wife went into labor on July 22, while writing our charter school application. She went to the hospital at 5:30 a.m. She begged the doctors to allow her to bring her laptop. The doctors replied no. We knew that the first delivery was laborious and figured this would be no different. To our surprise, my wife tried to deliver naturally, but the baby wasn't cooperating, so she was prepped for another Caesarean section. We then were told that the doctors needed to remove a thick layer of scar tissue from my wife's stomach. Plastic surgery now required, moving our completed charter school application out of reach. I refused to believe that we were being kicked down again. Our baby was finally born at 7:30 p.m. on July 22.

My wife could feel my disappointment about the unfinished charter application. She told me to bring her the laptop so she could finish the document. She completed our charter application the very next day. I overnighted it. The charter application arrived in Austin safely and on time.

Within two months of submittal, we received a confirmation and some changes. On the way to celebrate my wife's birthday on September 12, we received a call from the Texas Education Agency, informing us that the charter application was approved. We received our charter school contract in October 1998. FOCUS Learning Academy opened its doors on August 17, 1999 to 100 Kindergarten to 6th grade students on the second floor of a southern Dallas church.

The Need

In 1997, a quarter of Texan schoolchildren were unable to read at their respective grade levels. One in four, or 350,000 Texan schoolchildren, who took the state reading test failed. Of these children, 90,000 were third and fourth graders. (Texas Essential Knowledge and Skills 2007-2018) These facts indicated that an urgent need for the Texan educational school system to return to the basics of teaching children to read. At the heart of all FOCUS programs were the goal to teach all children to read.

Once children fall behind in reading, school problems can develop that are hard and costly to correct. Research shows that many students who are academically disadvantaged in a conventional classroom will experience lingering academic failure due to unidentified and/or unremedied learning disabilities. Their sense of self-worth and ability to accomplish their life goals will be forever damaged or possibly lost. Studies have shown that the impact of this loss isn't only detrimental to the person but also to society as a whole. In fact, 1 out of every 6 adults in the U.S. lack basic reading skills – that means 36 million people can't read a job application, understand basic written instructions, or read the Internet. (Final Adult Basic Education Fact Sheet Updated 2017)

These students grow up to become functionally illiterate adults who can potentially cost $300.8 billion a year through welfare, crime, health, job incompetence, remedial education costs, and lost taxes. (The-Economic -Social-Cost-of-Illiteracy 2015)

Our charter school's vision was to serve children with undiagnosed or diagnosed learning disabilities in a tuition-free school. Seventy-five percent of these students were identified as belonging to one of two categories under the Texas Education Code (TEC):

1. They already met eligibility criteria as an LD student outlined under IDEA, Section 504 of the Rehabilitation Act of 1973, and the Texas Education Agency.
2. They were determined to be at-risk based on Texas Education Code (TEC) Section 29.081 (d) 2a, b, which is as follows: a) did not perform satisfactorily on a readiness test or assessment instrument administered at the beginning of the school year, b) did not perform satisfactorily on an assessment instrument administered under Subchapter B, Chapter 39.

According to the FOCUS Learning Academy charter school application, our educational program was designed to perform the following:

- Stimulate the development of innovative special education programs.
- Provide opportunities for innovative learning and assessments for children considered as "learning-different" and at-risk.
- Provide parents and students with awareness and resources for learning disabilities within the school, local, state, and national sources.
- Provide teachers with tools for working at a school with alternative and innovative methods of educational instruction and school structure and management.
- Encourage performance-based educational programs for learning-different and at-risk children.
- Hold teachers and school administrators accountable for the educational outcomes of students.

Dallas Charter School Goals

The services of FLA-Texas would be rendered without discrimination or segregation due to race, creed, color, gender, or national origin. The goals of our program were as follows:

- Provide classroom settings that are structured in an environment to reduce distractions to a minimum and provide specialized instruction.
- Present a coordinated multisensory curriculum designed to develop the symbolic tools (reading, writing, spelling, speaking, listening, and math) necessary to gain, retain, and express information.
- Prepare students for a return to a conventional classroom setting.
- Develop and present a curriculum that increases awareness in social studies and science; provides experiences aimed at cultivating aesthetic values and recreational skills through art, music, and sports; and offers lessons to teach students how to develop, use, and care for one's body through physical education and perceptual motor skills.
- Create an atmosphere conducive to emotional health—feelings of success, fairness, concern, and respect for one's self and others—through training and social-skills promotion.
- Empower parents to support and advocate for their children by providing explanation and training about the child's learning abilities and challenges. Explanation and training will include information on comorbid conditions.

The Targeted Student Area

FLA-Texas targeted for instruction students from 23 surrounding school districts in the Dallas metropolitan area. At least 35 percent of these students were classified as at risk for school failure and having learning disabilities (including dyslexia, ADHD, and/or language processing problems) that had affected their ability to master grade-level reading skills.

The largest home or default school district from which FLA-Texas drew 65 percent of its students and those on its waiting list was the Dallas Independent School District (DISD). An analysis of the past three years of academic data revealed that 45 percent of the schools in this southern sector of Dallas were low-performing schools with an unacceptable rating for at least one out of three years and at least one-third received unacceptable rating three out of three years. Clearly, Dallas's high schools were failing.

Academic Structure

The charter school's design consisted of a multisensory program as the cornerstone of its curriculum, which was effective for all types of children from gifted students to those with special needs. However, the learning model was designed to work individually for LD children who were at risk of failure due to reading challenges. The school's model delivered instruction utilizing multisensory structured techniques. The grade-level-appropriate content was intertwined throughout the curriculum and tailored to meet state standards. The emphasis was placed on the multisensory instruction of reading, phonics, language arts, mathematics, science, social studies, and physical education focusing on fine motor skills.

The school's central objective was to teach LD children to read and foster a love of reading through daily instruction using the FOCUS Phonics Reading Program developed by the Texas Scottish Rite Hospital for Children. This success-based program had been validated by numerous research agencies and had a proven track record in teaching LD children to read. Also, traditional learners were taught phonics through programs such as Saxon Phonics (especially K–third grade students) along with Reading Mastery and Open Court programs.

Also, intensive special education in the mainstream classroom and speech-therapy services were a central part of the school's model. All subjects and programs were also aligned with Texas Essential Knowledge and Skills (TEKS), the state's standards for public schools from Kindergarten to 12th grades. TEKS detail the curriculum requirements for every course. State-mandated standardized tests, which measure the acquisition of specific knowledge and skills, are also outlined in the state's curriculum.

We implemented our educational model of timely and early identification of learning disabilities (as early as kindergarten). Trained professionals administered assessments with the proper tools and provided remediation with an emphasis on individualized and structured academics and self-csteem. Other components of the model included parent and community support, including school and community involvement with trained teachers and other professionals with specific expertise and experience in the field of learning disabilities, as well as available resources to help expand our programs.

Unlike schools that offered reading recovery programs, FLA-Texas was the only charter school that placed a strong emphasis on reading. Because children cannot recover from reading difficulties when they've not learned to read in the first place, we started each child at the bottom. Each student was then brought along gradually using a multisensory teaching program involving 180 minutes of daily instruction in phonics, language arts, and reading. We also offered a safe and orderly learning environment shaped by research-proven strategies such as Robert Murzano's nine high-yield strategies. Because many of the students were classified as at risk, a literacy-rich classroom environment was critical. Another tool used in the school's success was the creation of a Personalized Education Plan (PEP) for every child that included their pace, level, and content geared toward their specific ability, interests, and learning styles.

FOCUS Learning Academy—Conway, Arkansas

For Arkansas native Sammy, the struggle with reading began during his elementary years and should have been corrected by the time he was in middle school. Although Sammy wasn't identified as an LD child, he remained in high school and graduated with his cohorts.

In 2003, the memories of Sammy's academic challenges led the FOCUS Centre of Learning, Inc., to expand its educational program into the neighboring state of Arkansas, specifically in his hometown of Conway. The Arkansas Department of Education granted a charter school to FOCUS Learning Academy for Kindergarten to 6th grades. In August 2004, the doors opened to 100 students in a community church. This expanded sister school consistently remained academically strong in Arkansas' rating system.

Arkansas Achievement

In 2002, Arkansas remained at or near the bottom by every standard measure of student achievement when compared with other states on universally accepted academic performance tests such as the NAEP, ACT, SAT9. Sadly, Arkansas had the fourth highest U.S. illiteracy rate. (Barth and Nitta 2008, Ritter 2002, Annual Statistical Report Public Schools of Arkansas and Educational Service Cooperatives 2002)

- At least 30 percent of adult population in Arkansas was functionally or totally illiterate.
- More than 45 percent of Arkansas adults didn't have a high school diploma.
- One out of every four students who entered first grade did not graduate.

The Governor's Commission on Adult Literacy reported that "adult illiteracy costs Arkansas $23 million annually in public assistance, crime, unrealized tax revenues, and remedial reading programs." Research substantiated the fact that a high level of adult illiteracy was the end-product of an educational system failing to provide appropriate reading instruction for the neediest of students during the critical elementary years. (Miles to Go, Arkansas 2002, Barth and Nitta 2008)

The Target Area

Sammy wasn't alone in his struggles to read. Sadly, Conway and the surrounding area weren't immune from the harmful effects of reading failure.

Arkansas District Performance Reports (2000–2001) indicated that approximately 4-in-10 students in the target area had failed to master fourth-grade reading skills. The results of these reports follow:

Area District	General Population % At/Above Proficient Level	Combined Population % At/Above Proficient Level
Conway	60%	52%
Guy-Perkins	50%	42%
Mayflower	40%	42%
Mt. Vernon-Enola	55%	47%
Vilonia	63%	51%
Pulaski County	40%	35%

An estimated 40–60 percent of all local students were failing to master basic reading skills. And, when the special needs portion of the student population was included in the combined test results, district averages generally declined by more than six percentage points, indicating that many at-risk students were experiencing even less success in learning to read.

The gap in all measures of success for minority students also remained a worrisome factor. Although great strides had been made, African-American students still scored lower on all measures of achievement and showed a seven-point gap in the graduation rate when compared to white students. Clearly, more needed to be done to identify and serve these students within the context of the local community.

The FOCUS Educational Model

The FOCUS program was based upon the following principles:

- **High Expectations**— To achieve the desired goal of success for all students, the school held high expectations for all students, and especially for the special needs learner. The school viewed these students as having strengths, not deficits, and adopted programs and practices to help all students achieve their real potential.
- **Prompt Identification**— All students were extensively assessed upon entry into the school to determine their academic strengths and weaknesses and assisted in designing their academic program.
- **Targeted Remediation**— Every student had a Personalized Educational Program (PEP) designed to specify and target their diagnosed strengths and weaknesses. This program was in addition to the mandated IEP for special education students, and the AIP mandated for students who scored unacceptably on the Arkansas Benchmark test.
- **Ongoing Support**— The school offered extensive special services (including special education and speech) designed to meet the needs of all learners within the mainstream classroom. Teachers were extensively supported through the provision of specialized training in all content areas, focusing on the needs of LD learners.
- **Parent Involvement**— As a school of choice, FLA remained responsive to the vital role that parents play in their child's education and provided extensive educational and involvement opportunities to each parent. This extended community partnership designed to increase the effectiveness of its programs and services.

The FOCUS FLAME Program

At the heart of the charter school was the FOCUS Learning Academy Multisensory Education (FLAME) Program, which was designed by the school's leadership. In all core-content subjects, and extending to enrichment areas, the goal of the FLAME program was to encourage learners to engage in their learning process. With an emphasis on individualized instruction, the FLAME model incorporated the best of proven research-based curricula and teaching techniques, which had demonstrated success in working with both the regular and special-needs learner. But unlike other models, the FLAME program provided additional training and support services to maintain the special-needs learner in the mainstream classroom.

The school's curriculum for all grades emphasized the FLAME-teaching approach of research-proven theories and practices for children with reading disabilities, including various language-processing problems and utilization of multisensory activities. Students learn to use and remember information best when they are taught with activities that utilize all the senses (visual, auditory, and kinesthetic). The curriculum deliberately engaged all three pathways to enable each student's strongest modality, which led to the development of their weaker modalities. The curriculum prepared students with the skills and knowledge necessary to successfully complete high school, college, or other instructional programs, as well as to enter the workforce ready for the challenges they would face. The curricula were aligned to the Arkansas Curriculum Frameworks.

In addition, the FOCUS FLAME curriculum also included a heavy emphasis on assessment, which provided the information necessary for improving student performance through instructional decision-making, goal-setting, and resource allocation, in addition to accountability to their parents, the community, and the mandated requirements of the Arkansas Comprehensive Testing, Assessment, and Accountability Program and federal education authorities. The FLAME model included the FOCUS AP program, a multisensory, structured method of reading, handwriting, and spelling instruction developed by the Texas Scottish Rite Hospital for Children for use with both regular-education students and those with language-processing deficits. (Multisensory teaching of basic language skills 2018)

Like its sister school in Texas, reading consisted of the FOCUS Phonics Program, which was used in daily, 1-hour small group sessions as a basic language curriculum, both to remediate deficiencies and provide a strong foundation for reading in all subject areas. A state-provided reading, language arts, literature, and spelling curriculum was also used during an additional language arts/reading session to provide standards-based grade-level instruction to all students.

Other curriculum components included Multisensory Math, which emphasized the hands-on nature of mathematics instruction using multisensory teaching approaches that activated two or more learning pathways simultaneously. The program emphasized a balanced approach to teaching number sense, properties, and operations; measurement; geometry and spatial sense; data analysis and statistics; and algebra and functions math; developing practical problem-solving skills; and reviewing concepts systematically to support a variety of learning styles. The FLAME Model of hands-on learning and inquiry-based instructional techniques were taught in social studies, science, and even enrichment activities. All lesson plans were broken down by element and grade-level objectives in correspondence with the Arkansas Curriculum Frameworks for all subjects.

As inclusive of the philosophical basis of the FOCUS Centre of Learning's premise for working with the special-needs child, all teachers were required to attend a two-week (70-hour) preservice workshop to master the basic concepts of the FOCUS AP program. Ongoing training included eight Saturday sessions and four professional observations throughout the school year, with teachers eligible to apply for certification as an Academic Language Therapist after completing the requirements of the two-year masters-level program.

Iconic Programs for Two Schools

Power Hour—Reading for All

Using FOCUS Centre of Learning, Inc.'s staple programs of alphabetic phonics and the Orton-Gillingham teacher training model, the two schools had a level playing field with specialized programs especially for learning disabled students. Those two programs were iconic for the charter school movement because no other schools offered such programs.

The success of our schools started with FOCUS Phonics in a one-hour program designated school-wide in what we called the Power Hour. This zero period was conducted from 8 a.m.-9 a.m. every day with fidelity. The guidelines for teaching FOCUS Phonics were as follows:

- Present all new material through the three primary channels: visual, auditory, and kinesthetic.
- Structure each procedure, numbering the steps that the students must follow and require them to use these steps repeatedly in precisely the same order.
- Provide challenging activities that require repetition of all fundamental processes until automaticity is achieved.
- In planning, reduce any material to be taught to its smallest elements and organize these elements sequentially.
- Give all instructions or directions by telling, showing, and helping students to "walk through," "talk through," "draw through," or otherwise to rehearse them to ensure their full understanding;

- Assume nothing and ask students to perform only those tasks for which they have the right tools, and start at the beginning and take ongoing inventory, checking their knowledge in pertinent areas as you go.
- Measure the students' progress in all areas throughout training—never move on to a new concept until 95 percent of the material has been learned.
- Teach thoroughly the important arbitrary learning that cannot be discovered or inducted, such as the alphabet sequence and the basic sound-symbol relationships.
- Prepare to be flexible and creative in approaching each student and in persisting until every student is able to grasp and then use the material.
- Plan each day's lesson to ensure that the students achieve both near-perfect success and awareness that they've explained their knowledge by another step, even if it's a small one.

Every student was given a modified version of benchmark measures called FOCUS Benchmark Assessment, which was originally developed by the Texas Scottish Rite Hospital staff. Our trained teachers administered the benchmark measures at intervals throughout daily instruction to periodically determine the amount of growth in learning since the last measurement. The FOCUS Benchmark Assessment tool was part of our continuous progress monitoring for reading/language. Although it didn't conform to a nationally recognized standardized test, the measurement tool could also be modified and used as a national assessment for all children.

Progress Monitoring

The FOCUS Benchmark Assessment tool was based on lessons within the alphabetic phonics curriculum. We couldn't move forward if a child hadn't successfully mastered at least 90 percent of that schedule. Also, it measured the progress in reading and reading comprehension, as well as to conduct periodic accountability reviews for each student's progress. The progress of each child was charted daily and weekly on a Monthly Graphemes Schedule to determine where he/she was progressing in the schedule of lessons and activities. Teachers also provided a formal initial, mid-term, and final Progress Report, which explained how the student's responses pointed to their particular strengths and weaknesses involving the findings during each timeframe.

Attendance

Because the FOCUS Phonics program was very structured, sequential, and accumulative, perfect attendance was highly recommended, so we monitored the children's attendance as well. Also, Incentives for increasing and maintaining high attendance were promoted.

Specialized Teaching as an Academic Language Therapist

As we've discussed, not all children learn traditionally, and many teachers instruct students as they've learned or were taught themselves. The FOCUS Phonics Program engaged all learning modalities (visual, auditory, and kinesthetic [muscle movement]) and addressed every learning style. Research has proven that most students need from 1 to 28 exposures to a concept before that concept is actually learned, (Horst 2013) Meaningful repetition was built-in automatically in the FOCUS Phonics Program, which was structured, systematic, and cumulative to ensure the student's learning.

Each school used the FOCUS Teacher Training Program, which was the habilitative or rehabilitative instruction of the student with language-based learning difficulties. Our teacher training model prepared our regular education classroom teachers to be teachers in academic therapy through the Orton-Gillingham theories and techniques. Under the tutelage of a qualified instructor or master teacher, the training program consisted of structured procedures and a sequential presentation of all material. These requirements were especially designed for converting defeated children into capable, confident, success-oriented, productive citizens.

The benefits to having every teacher trained as a Certified Academic Language Therapist (CALT) empowered teachers to help restore the children's confidence and reverse their poor self-images. Additional benefits for a CALT are as follows:

- Satisfied their practicum obligation through the daily instruction of students in the school's Power Hour, which was a school-wide one-hour skill-building class for every student.
- Understood and developed insights into the academic problems of their students, in addition to the social-emotional, behavioral, and often health problems that accompany learning disabilities and reading difficulties.

- Coached students in learning strategies and study skills for handling assignments; organizing, planning, and completing writing and long-range projects; and test taking.
- Understood the formal and informal assessments reports of students, psychological and language assessments, and educational achievement tests.
- Trained in the protocols of case management, recordkeeping, report writing, communication with parents and other professionals, interaction with school personnel, confidentiality, and ethical conduct .
- Completed two years of extensive coursework in knowledge domain of the aspects of the underlying neurophysiology and neuropsychology (brain function), psychology (personality development), psycholinguistics (cognition and language), genetics (heritability), phonology, language development and disorders, education, and research relevant to the diagnosis and treatment of language-based learning difficulties.
- Required practicum hours.
- Required licensure by a nationally recognized professional organization.

Since its program inception, six teachers became CALTs through our Centre, while countless others who left either the Centre's program or FOCUS Learning Academy to teach in other school districts were certified through other ALTA training programs.

Language Science Department

The Language Science Department was established to provide direction instruction for students who struggle with reading, spelling and writing. The department implements evidence-based curricula developed at Texas Scottish Rite Hospital for Children in Dallas, Texas. Both programs, Alphabetic Phonics and Take Flight, included the components of reading instruction identified in the 2000 report by the National Reading Panel as consistently related to reading success. Those five areas of reading instruction are phonemic awareness, phonics, fluency, vocabulary and text comprehension. The Language Science Department was responsible for the oversight of the FOCUS Teacher Training program.

FOCUS Learning Academy Comparison Chart

Mission Statement

The mission statement of the school was *"The stakeholders of FOCUS Academies will provide world-class, innovative and multisensory educational experiences that inspire all students to achieve positive life goals with global impact."*

FOCUS Learning Academy, Texas and Arkansas campuses, were a school of choice that provided an academic atmosphere for the learning disabled and at-risk child as well as the traditional learner. Recognizing each child's individual talents and strengths, the model at FOCUS was designed to deliver instruction and activities utilizing multisensory, structured techniques.

Both charter schools identified learning disabilities unashamedly as the heart and soul of its charter application. Our academic approach provided early intervention and specialized teaching from prekindergarten age four through high school for students who were identified or undiagnosed with reading difficulties. Our school's model combined purposeful and strategic activities with trained teachers who understood a student's learning disabilities and abilities. A comparison of both schools provides an overview of a comprehensive education program for all students. Ninety-eight percent of our students were taught in the mainstream setting.

The FOCUS model embodied the resources and proven practices necessary to ensure that every child is challenged to reach his/her fullest potential. We offered the following:

- An emphasis on early identification of learning disabilities
- Multisensory approach to teaching to reading/writing/spelling, language, and math
- Full integrated special needs services including a Diagnostic and Evaluation and Speech-Language services
- Highly trained specialists and professionals in the area of learning disabilities
- Structured and effective Special Education Program
- Warm, supportive atmosphere where bright minds have the opportunity to thrive
- We promoted remediation and successful modifications in the mainstream classroom

Extensive and on-going training for professionals in the field of learning differences.

Structure	Texas	Arkansas
Operational Dates	August 1999–August 31, 2017	August 2003–June 30, 2007
Grades Served	Pre-Kindergarten 4 year olds–12th grade	Kindergarten–6th grade
Student Demographics	African American: 93%, Anglo: 3%, Hispanic: 4%	African American: 95%, Anglo: 3%, Hispanic: 2%
Economically Disadvantaged	90%	70%
Special Education Students	35% (90% of special-education students mainstreamed)	20% (90% of special-education students mainstreamed)
School Type	Charter school	Charter school
Teacher/Student Ratio	24:1	15:1
Research-based methods and strategies	Basic skills with emphasis on FOCUS Phonics	Basic skills with emphasis on FOCUS Phonics; FOCUS Learning Academy Multisensory Education (FLAME)
Comprehensive design with aligned components	FLAME (FOCUS Learning Academy Multisensory Education) Effective school functioning, including instruction, assessment, classroom management, professional development, parental involvement, and school management designed to enable *all* students—including those from low-income families and LD children—to meet challenging state content and performance standards	Same design
FLA Uniqueness	<ul><li>The *only* charter school that placed strong emphasis on reading</li><li>The *only* charter school with *all* teachers trained to become certified as an Academic Language Therapists</li><li>The *only* charter school to integrate an AP Orton-Gillingham method for teaching LD children into its daily curriculum with a required one-hour program taught in all classrooms</li><li>One of few charter schools to target students with learning challenges and other special academic needs—the 20% of students often neglected in other schools</li><li>Mainstreamed *most* of its LD students into regular classrooms with a trained Academic Language Therapist</li></ul>	

Trestan was a third grader in 1997. He failed the TAAS test. Like Trestan, hundreds of children in public schools have never been assessed for a learning disability promptly nor can they afford private after-school academic services. They've missed an opportunity to receive the necessary support to achieve success in school. An assessment process is to determine how to make informed decisions about the educational placement and instruction for many children. Also, many of these disadvantaged children need trained reading teachers to provide specific reading programs and accommodations in their public-school settings.

In 1997, the Texas Education Agency reported that 43% of the third graders required extra instructional assistance, such as mentoring or tutoring, to help master the Grade 3 curriculum. On average, students who received extra assistance had lower TAAS scores and were reported to have mastered fewer of the Essential Elements than other third graders in the study. Students referred by their teachers for special education assessment (11%) or language assessment (10%) were more likely to demonstrate lower levels of performance, as well. (Snapshot '97: 1996-97 School District Profiles 1997)

After serving LD students through FOCUS Centre of Learning, we had to do more to impact students in an all-day full-time academic setting. The population we served could not afford tuition or transportation to a specialized private school in far North Dallas. As a result, we thought outside of the box and developed a school of choice called a public charter school in two states. The tuition-free charter schools were structured similarly to a private school where students wore uniforms and a specialized reading programs designed for students with learning disabilities. The schools received funding from state formula allotments and federal competitive and noncompetitive grants.

FOCUS Centre of Learning and FOCUS Learning Academy cared enough to start small programs eventually expanding to multiple campuses with schools in two states. It must not stop there for serving students with learning disabilities. This school brought hope and new life to the community. More importantly, parents had a viable school choice at no cost for their child (ren). Students and parents from downtrodden neighborhoods started taking pride and ownership in their new school's success. The schools in both states exhibited success by students displaying academic progress in all subjects, especially in reading.

In a climate of budgetary concerns and in light of a growing student population riddled with underachievement, the problems of students who fail to achieve their potential but function below or near-grade level doesn't alarm most educators. Who cares about Trestan and the other children like him who suffer from undiagnosed or diagnosed learning or reading disabilities?

The African-American community can be remediated as a vibrant community by fighting off the growth of illiteracy and high crime. To educate at-risk youth to their maximum potential, educators, the community, and community leaders must collaborate and demonstrate a strong commitment to the education of at-risk youth if other citizens are to follow. If timely identification and remediation programs aren't provided for LD youth, they likely will become functionally illiterate adults, contributing to the exorbitant billion-dollar cost annually through welfare, crime, job incompetence, remedial education costs, and lost taxes. Answers to the nation's growing crime problems lie not with the government, but in the home and community. America must invest in its children and help them to build character and moral strength, rather than building more prisons to house them in.

In summary, helping struggling students can't just stop with programs such as FOCUS Centre of Learning or FOCUS Learning Academy. Parents, teachers and administrators can and must do more jointly. With a leap of faith and a plan, schools and organizations can serve thousands of students who are dyslexic, LD and ADHD. We need educational institutions and organizations to become a beacon of light to underserved highly populated minority communities. With a sample action plan in our last chapter, *How Sammy Can Learn to Read-A Service Delivery Plan*, anyone can implement a program for struggling readers who can find academic success and thrive with newfound freedom on their educational journey.

Chapter 8
Thriving with Abilities

Learning disabilities, dyslexia, or ADHD. Have you heard of them? Do you know anyone who has one or two of these learning challenges? Chances are very good that you do. In 2017, the World Health Organization reported that more than 1 billion people in the world are estimated to live with some form of a disability. This corresponds to about 15% of the world's population. (Fact Sheet: Disability and health 2018)

While some disabilities are visible, such as a person in a wheelchair, other are invisible. Like an individual who has a learning disability, even though you cannot see a person's disability, it doesn't mean they don't have one. Because many famous and great people are well-known for a disability, I like to simply call them abilities. In fact, some of the biggest names in sports, business, movie, entertainment, and politics have made major contributions to our country despite their learning disabilities.

This chapter cover some of these individuals who found their passion and turned their challenges in major contributions to our world. Our intent is to focus more on the giftedness of these famous individuals who overcame obstacles and even propelled them to successful and notable careers. Let's examine the works of the hands of some famous people who struggled with a learning disability.

#1 The Dyslexic Billionaire Club

Need further proof that LD students can be successful? As of 2016, 22 billionaires have been identified as dyslexic. Check out how they overcame their struggles by creating world-renowned businesses and other contributions to the world. (22 Dyslexic Billionaires n.d.)

Sir Richard Branson-"If I'm not interested in something, I don't grasp it."

Net worth: $5.1 billion

Dyslexic billionaire's source of wealth: The Virgin Group

When Branson was in school, many of his teachers considered him stupid and lazy. "I was dyslexic, I had no understanding of schoolwork whatsoever. I certainly would have failed IQ tests. And it as one of the reasons I left school when I was 15 years old. And if I..."

Warren Buffett-"Someone is sitting in the shade today because someone planted a tree a long time ago."

Net worth: $72.7 billion

Dyslexic billionaire's source of wealth: Being the most successful investor in the world

According to the *Washington Post*, school was a problem for Buffet. He was so bored in class and so eager to pursue his business ideas. The only teacher who got through to him was the school's golf coach. He also enjoyed his newspaper routes as a paper boy. He had so any routes that his annual income was greater than that of his teachers.

John Chambers-"I cannot explain why, but I just approach problems differently."

Net worth: $1 billion

Dyslexic billionaire's source of wealth: CISCO

For a long time, the CEO of Cisco kept his dyslexia a secret, but over the past decade he's worked to make his difficulty with reading more public.

Henry Ford

Net worth: $199 billion (today's estimated worth)

Dyslexic billionaires source of wealth: Ford Motor Company

Ford used his dyslexia to his advantage. He would repeat certain actions over and over and use rote learning to remember things. From this experience, he transformed the auto industry around the world by introducing the idea of the assembly line. Don't find fault, find a remedy."

Bill Gates-"I failed in some subjects in exam, but my friend passed in all. Now he is an engineer in Microsoft and I am the owner of Microsoft."

Net Worth: $79.2 billion

Billionaire's source of wealth: Microsoft

Gates was branded a dunce—a person incapable of learning—at school and it seemed his dyslexia felled him at every step. Computers took that hurdle away with a single click of the mouse and the launch of the Spell Check application. Today, he's the wealthiest man in the world with a net worth of $79 billion dollars. Gates founded Microsoft after dropping out of college.

Reyn Guyer

Net worth: $4.4 billion (today's estimated worth)

Billionaire's source of wealth: Being the creator of the NERF ball and TWISTER

Guyer struggled with basic reading problems and writing as a child. He didn't find out about his diagnosis until one of his daughters was diagnosed in the teenage years. All of a sudden while listening to the results of her educational assessment, he realized that the psychologist was describing his own difficulties.

Bill Hewlett-"The greatest success goes to the person who is not afraid to fail in front of even the largest audience."

New worth: $9 billion (today's estimated worth)

Dyslexic billionaire's source of wealth: The Hewlett-Packard Company (HP)

Considered one of the founding fathers of Silicon Valley and the American electronics industry, William Hewlett, with his friend and partner David Packard, began his career in electronic development in a garage in the 1930s. Hewlett's early academic career was initially unimpressive, hampered by undiagnosed dyslexia, which gave him difficulty with written material and writing assignments but led him to develop exceptional memorization and logical skills. Hewlett excelled in mathematics and sciences, which, with his father's tenure at Stanford, helped him enter the university in 1930.

Steve Jobs-"Here's to the crazy ones. The misfits. The rebels. The troublemakers. The round pegs in the square holes."

Net worth: $19 billion (today's estimated worth)

Dyslexic billionaire's source of wealth: Apple

The late Steve Jobs struggled in school. From his early days in elementary school where he grew frustrated with formal schooling, to college where he dropped out after just one semester. Jobs didn't like school because he didn't believe it had practical application in his life.

"The ones who see things differently. They're not fond of rules. And they have no respect for the status quo. You can quote them, disagree with them, glorify or vilify them. About the only thing you cannot do is ignore them. Because they change things. They push the human race forward. And while so may see them as the crazy ones, we see genius. Because the people who are crazy enough to think they can change the world, are ones who do."

Ingvar Kamprad-"Only those who are asleep make no mistakes."

Net worth: $3.4 billion

Dyslexic billionaire's source of wealth: IKEA

Normally, products are identified by some kind of code, which gives indications about the nature and origin of an item, but only to an educated user. However, as Ingvar Kamprad had dyslexia, he had difficulties with any sort of code. This led to a situation where he had difficulties remembering the order numbers of his own products. Instead of ignoring or delegating this issue, he came up with a creative idea to use names instead of code. Wardrobes and hall furniture were named after Norwegian places. Chairs and desks received men's name. Materials and curtains received women's names, and garden furniture was identified by the names of Swedish Islands. Kamprad's solution to his problem provides interesting insights into his personality as a leader.

Craig McCaw- "Growing up, I had trouble fitting in.... As a dyslexic, I don't think like other people, so I didn't fit very well in a clique.

Net worth: $1.86 billion

Dyslexic billionaire's source of wealth: McCaw Cellular and Clearwire Corporation, a pioneer in the cellular phone industry

McCaw credits his ability to see circumstances from unique perspectives— to see, for example, the potential of cellular communications, an insight that seems obvious now but that was uncommon in its day—to the challenges of growing up dyslexic.

Dyslexia forced me to be quite conceptual, because I'm not very good at details ... and because I'm not good at details, I tend to be rather spatial in my thinking, oriented to things in general terms, rather than the specific. That allows you to step back and take in the big picture. I feel blessed about that."

O. D. McKee

Net worth: $1.5 billion

Dyslexic billionaire's source of wealth: McKee Foods Corporation

The founder of McKee Foods Corporation, O. D. never finished college due to his dyslexia. Still, it didn't stop him from founding a small bakery with his wife, that eventually turned into a hugely successful business.

David H. Murdock-"Everybody laughed at me, they thought I was an imbecile."

Net worth: $3.5 billion

Dyslexic billionaire's source of wealth: Being an American businessman

Murdock had dyslexia, though no one initially realized it. He never managed grades better than Ds and dropped out of school at age 14.

David Neeleman-"I knew I had strengths that other didn't have, and my parents reminded me of them when my teachers didn't see them ..."

Net worth: $1.6 billion

Dyslexic billionaire's source of wealth: Founder of four commercial airlines—Morris Air, Westjet, JetBlue Airways, and Azul Brazilian Airlines

"I can distill complicated facts and come up with simple solutions. I can look out on an industry with all kinds of problems and say, 'How can I do this better?'"

Kerry Packer-"A very wise old man who taught me about TV once told me if you can be right 60% of the time, you will own the world."

Net worth: $4.8 billion (estimated today's worth)

Dyslexic billionaire's source of wealth: Being an Australian media tycoon

Nelson Rockefeller-"For I was one of the "puzzle children'" myself—a dyslexic, or 'reverse reader'" —and I still have a hard time reading today..."

Net worth: $72.7 billion (today's estimated worth)

Dyslexic billionaire's source of wealth: Family money.

Businessman, philanthropist, public servant, and politician

"But after coping with this problem for more than 60 years, I have a message of encouragement for children with learning disabilities-and their parents. Based on my own experience, my message to dyslexic children is this: "Don't accept anyone's verdict that you are lazy, stupid, or retarded.' "

Charles Schwab-"It's painful. People decide you aren't working hard enough or are slow. I didn't quit, because I was really good in other things, terrific in math and science and anything that didn't deal with words. I was good in sports. I had good skills in dealing with people."

Net worth: $6.9 billion

Dyslexic billionaire's source of wealth: The Charles Schwab Corporation (brokerage and banking)

Schwab had extreme difficulty in taking notes in class and failed English two times. He also struggled in foreign-language classes but never had a name for his disability. It was only when his son was diagnosed with dyslexia that he realized he also had it. Schwab saw both sides of struggling with dyslexia, as a parent of a struggling dyslexic child and as a dyslexic himself.

Carlos Slim-"There are people who are good for letters, and there are others that are good for numbers.

Net worth: $72.9 billion

Dyslexic billionaire's source of wealth: Telecom

Kerry Stokes-"It's very hard work. Words are not my skill and because they're not my skill, I have to work doubly hard."

Net worth: $1.15 billion

Dyslexic billionaire's source of wealth: Being an Australian businessman

Young Stokes frequently felt the strap at school when he misspelt words and turned in poorly written work. His teachers could see that he was bright, so they assumed his disability, diagnosed decades later as dyslexia, was the product of laziness or disrespect. He left school at 14.

Richard C. Strauss-"I thought I was pretty dumb. ... It causes a lot of people to do what I did—get attention in other ways by being a disciplinary problem."

Net worth: $18.5 billion

Dyslexic billionaire's source of wealth: Real estate developing

Strauss was diagnosed as having dyslexia in high school and eventually dropped out of college after a year and a half to pursue his real estate career, thus "avoiding reading and writing, which I'm not good at". He said that at school he was always "right at the bottom of the class" and that he "failed a number of classes every year."

Lord Alan Sugar-"Don't tell me you're just like me. You're not like me. I'm unique."

Net worth: $2.01 billion

Dyslexic billionaire's source of wealth: Amstrad

Lord Sugar left school early to pursue his business interests, starting a market stall in London's East End. Dyslexia hasn't a barrier to success for him.

Ted Turner-"The mind is just another muscle."

Net worth: $2.2 billion

Dyslexic billionaire's source of wealth: Being the founder of Cable News Network (CNN)

Turner had difficulty in school. He soon discovered that certain subjects were challenging for him, such as math and reading, while others he grew to like. He demonstrated a nature talent for business.

William Wrigley Jr.- "Nothing great was ever achieved without enthusiasm."

Net worth: $2.6 billion

Dyslexic billionaire's source of wealth: Chewing gum

#2 Celebrities

Research shows that individuals with dyslexia tend to 1 earn through unconventional methods. Just ask David Boies, a celebrated trial attorney, best known as the guy who beat Microsoft. "It is a disability in learning," says Boies. "It is not an intelligence disability. It doesn't mean you can't think." Sally Shaywitz, a leading dyslexia neuroscientist at Yale, believes the disorder can carry surprising talents along with its well-known disadvantages. "Dyslexics are overrepresented in the top ranks of people who are unusually insightful, who bring a new perspective, who think out of the box," says Shaywitz. She is co-director of the Center for Learning and Attention at Yale, along with her husband, Dr. Bennett Shaywitz, a professor of pediatrics and neurology. (Morris, Resear and Neering 2002)

Boies joins a growing list of entrepreneurs, celebrities, presidents, and other famous and notable individuals who are known and some may even publicly speak about their learning disability. Here are just some of the individuals.

Actor/Actress: Tom Cruise is unable to read even today due to severe dyslexia. He never even finished high school. He has, though, the ability to memorize his lines and perform on both the stage and screen.

With all the lines that **Danny Glover** had to memorize and deliver as a famous actor, no one would suspect that a guidance counselor once described him as retarded in school. In the 1950s, he went undiagnosed as dyslexic.

Whoopi Goldberg was used to the kids calling her dumb. As an adult, she was later diagnosed with dyslexia. A comedian and a talk show host, she's one of only a dozen people to have won a Grammy, an Academy Award, an Emmy, and a Tony Award.

Being diagnosed with dyslexia as a teen didn't stop Mexican-born actress **Salma Hayek** from learning English and breaking into Hollywood as an adult. She admits to reading scripts very slowly but told WebMD, "I'm really a fast learner. I always was."

Formally diagnosed with ADHD as a teenager, **Roxy Olin**, of MTV's *The Hills* and *The City* fame, told *ADDitude* magazine, "I've learned, at this point in my life, that [ADHD] is a part of who I am. You don't have to keep your ADHD a secret." After struggling to fight distractions in school, Olin takes Adderall, sees a therapist, and uses organization and time-management strategies to keep her symptoms in check.

Dancer: *Dancing With The Stars* Karina Smirnoff has lived with ADHD her whole life, but it wasn't until a few years ago that she was properly diagnosed. After working with her doctor to find the best treatment for her inattention and impulsivity, she told *ABC News*, "[Vyvanse] helps me control my symptoms."

Musician: Adult with ADHD, **Phillip Manuel**, a New Orleans jazz musician, has never been one for a 9-to-5 desk job, but his creative spirit ended up being a professional and personal blessing. "He was always hands-on with [our] kids," his wife Janice told the Washington Post. "He went on field trips, helped with homework and class projects. All the teachers knew him." Always a bit impulsive, Manuel eventually started taking ADHD medication, something that has made the couple's relationship even smoother.

Singer: Singer/songwriter, actor, and entrepreneur, **Justin Timberlake** was diagnosed with ADHD as a child.

According to Health.com, **Solange Knowles**, sister of Beyonce, had to be diagnosed twice before she believed she had ADHD. "I didn't believe the first doctor who told me," Knowles said. "I guess I was in denial."

Dyslexia Celebrities: Actresses/Actors-Harry Belafonte, Toni Bennett, Orlando Bloom, George Burns, Johnny Depp, Harrison Ford, Tracey Gold, Woody Harrelson, Anthony Hopkins, Keira Knightley, Marilyn Monroe, Mary Tyler Moore, Jack Nicholson, Edward Olmos, Keanu Reeves, Sylvester Stallone, Vince Vaughn, Lindsay Wagner, Robin Williams, Henry Winkler; **Model-**Kendall Jenner; **Musicians-**Ludweig Beethoven, Adam Levine, Mozart, Ozzy Ozzbourne, Chris Robinson, Carla Simone; **Singer-**

John Lennon; **Singer/Actress**-Cher Bono; **Singer/Songwriter**-Florence Welch; **ADHD Celebrities: Actresses/Actors**-Erin Brockovich-Ellis, Jim Carrey, Ryan Goslin, Lindsey Lohan, Patrick McKenna, Roxy Olin, Mary -Kate Olsen, Channing Tatum; **Actor/Filmmaker**-Trudie Styler (ADHD/ Dyslexia); **Chef**-Jamie Oliver; **Singer**- Britney Spears (ADHD/Dyslexia)

Oscar Winners

Goldie Hawn: *Best Supporting Actress: Cactus Flower (1969)* Hawn has made a career of making people laugh. Her Academy Award–winning role in Cactus Flower was one of many in which she played a funny free spirit. However, as a child, she didn't experience such good times in the classroom. Hawn had dyslexia and struggled with reading comprehension. "School was difficult for me," Hawn has said. "However, I was a happy child, so I always signed my papers, 'Love, Goldie.'"

Dyslexia: Oscar Winning Actors/Actresses (Wright, 10 Oscar Winners With Dyslexia 2014-2018):

- Robert Benton **Best Director and Best Adapted Screenplay:** *Kramer vs. Kramer* **(1979) Best Original Screenplay:** *Places in the Heart* **(1984)**
- Goldie Hawn **Best Supporting Actress:** *Cactus Flower* **(1969)**
- John Irving **Best Adapted Screenplay:** *The Cider House Rules* **(1999)**
- Steve McQueen **Best Picture:** *12 Years a Slave* **(2013)**
- Octavia Spencer **Best Supporting Actress:** *The Help* **(2011)**
- Peggy Stern **Best Animated Short:** *Moon and the Son: An Imagined Conversation* **(2005)**
- Richard Taylor **Best Makeup and Best Visual Effects,** *The Lord of the Rings: The Fellowship of the Ring* **(2001) Best Makeup and Best Costume Design,** *The Lord of the Rings: The Return of the King* **(2003) Best Visual Effects,** *King Kong* **(2005)**
- Billy Bob Thornton **Best Adapted Screenplay:** *Sling Blade* **(1996)**
- Loretta Young **Best Actress:** *The Farmer's Daughter* **(1947)**
- Roger Ross Williams **Best Documentary (Short Subject):** *Music by Prudence* **(2009)**

#3 Entertainment

Comedian, Actor, and Game Show Host: **Howie Mandel**, who has attention deficit hyperactivity disorder (ADHD) and obsessive compulsive disorder

(OCD), publicly revealed his diagnoses to the world on an impulse. An admission he regretted immediately afterward (sound familiar?) — until he realized just how many other people suffered from a combination of ADHD, OCD, and other comorbid conditions.

Film Director: Legendary film director, **Steven Spielberg** wasn't diagnosed with dyslexia until he was in his 60s. School administrators simply thought he was lazy.

Producers: Walt Disney was considered to be a slow student and didn't have a successful school experience. He became an internationally famous well-known movie producer and cartoonist.

Writer: Hans Christian Anderson was a young boy who had difficulty reading, but he was a successful writer who write some of the world's best-loved stories.

Dyslexia Entertainment: Comedian-Eddie Izzard; **TV Personality**-Jay Leno; **ADHD Entertainment: Entertainer**-Evel Kinevel; **TV Personality**-Ty Pennington

#4 Entrepreneurs

Albert Black is a Dallas businessman and multimillionaire who was born and raised in South Dallas with Dyslexia. Albert grew up living in the low-income government-subsidized housing projects known as the Dallas Housing Authority (DHA). He was determined to rise out of the projects with his outstanding work ethics. Black isn't only a successful businessman with several business ventures, but he's now the DHA chairman. (Black 2017)

Daymond John started his own successful clothing line called FUBU, is a star on *Shark Tank*, and has dyslexia. Growing up, his mom encouraged him to read. John and his mother have spoken about his lightbulb moment when he figured out he had dyslexia. His mom had him doing puzzles early in his childhood, so he could work on focusing. She also had him to read out loud, so that he would more focus on reading the word, instead of skipping over it. John eventually turned a $40 budget into FUBU, a $6 billion fashion game-changer.

Known as the best professional basketball player ever, **Michael Jordan** is now NBA team owner. He's has been cited as having ADHD. Jordan has a very successful Jordan marketing brand. He wasn't only one of the most successful athletes on the court, but he's also successful off the court in the world of business. He could be the only athlete worth over a billion dollars with his Jordan brand making him one of the richest athletes in the world. His net worth is over $1.3 billion dollars.

Will Smith, one of the most successful actors, comedians, entertainers and businessmen, attributes his success over the years to two things: His inability to read and the fact that his girlfriend cheated on him because she thought he wasn't good enough because he couldn't read. Will has dyslexia. He once sat at a desk and felt helpless due to his inability to understand the written word.

Dyslexia Entrepreneur: Developer (Apple)-Jonathan Ive; **ADHD Entrepreneur: Businesswoman**-Paris Hilton

#5 Leaders

Author/Journalist: Though she struggled academically, writing gave journalist and author **Katherine Ellison** a chance to excel. Diagnosed at 49, after her son was diagnosed as having ADHD.

Inventors/Scientists: Alexander Graham Bell was the inventor of the lightbulb.

Thomas Edison was unable to read until he was 12 years old, and his writing skills were poor throughout his life.

Albert Einstein was one of the persons who were gifted with a high level of intelligence. He became known as a great thinker and a super intelligent scientist. He actually changed the viewpoint of mankind about the universe. He contributed a lot in the field of science but despite his success as a scientist, he suffered from learning disability. During his time, he was diagnosed with dyslexia, autism and attention deficit disorder. But, he was able to overcome all of these challenges as he excelled and gained respect and recognition for all of his accomplishments as a scientist.

News Anchor: **Anderson Cooper** hasn't let dyslexia stand in the way of his success. He also won't allow his reading issues to stand in the way of his love for books and literature. His own book, Dispatches from the Edge: A Memoir of War, Disasters, and Survival, was on The New York Times best-seller list.

Political analyst, commentator, and educator: **James Carville** may have helped former President Bill Clinton win his 1992 White House bid, but Carville's ADHD — the condition that keeps him hyperfocused, adaptable, and full of the sort of excess energy politics demands.

Real Estate: **Barbara Corcoran** says her mom found ways to reframe her struggles with reading. "My mother rephrased dyslexia as a gift in my mind early on," Corcoran says. "She constantly told me when I didn't do well in school not to worry about it. Her attitude was, 'You have a wonderful imagination and you'll fill in the blanks.'" How grateful was Corcoran for that advice? One of her book is titled *Use What You've Got and Other Business Lessons I Learned From My Mom.—The Corcoran Group*

TV Journalist: Award-winning TV journalist Lisa Ling struggled in school from the time she was a child all the way through college. She eventually dropped out of college, went on to become a producer, special correspondent and, eventually, an investigative journalist with her own show. While reporting on ADHD, she discovered that her own struggles are because she, too, has ADHD. It was a relief and allowed her to look at herself in a new way. "In a strange way I do feel like it has helped me. I can hyperfocus on things that I am excited and passionate about," she has said.

TV/Radio Personality: **Glenn Beck** has found relief from his ADHD by taking Vyvanse. Though he credits his success to his condition, he joked in an interview with Ty Pennington, where the two discussed ADHD on *The Glenn Beck Show*, that his show staff members know when he hasn't taken his medication.

Writer: Hans Christian Anderson was a young boy who had difficulty reading, but he was a successful writer who write some of the world's best-loved stories.

Dyslexia Leaders: Artist-Pablo Picasso; **Business**-John Chambers; **Designer**-Tommy Hilfiger; **Lawyer**-David Boies; **Photographer**-David Bailey; **Writers**-Agatha Christie, F. Scott Fitzgerald; **ADHD Leaders: Artist**-Leonardo Da Vinci (ADHD/Dyslexia); **Businessman**- Paul Orfalea; **Media**-Alan Meckler; **Philosopher**-Socrates; **Talent Agency**-Ari Emanuel; **Writer**-Edger Allan Poe

#6 Military/Political

Winston Churchill was a noted Englishman who had much difficulty in school. He later became a national leader and an English Prime Minister. He became one of the best political leaders during the 20th century and he was even recognized as the savior of the world. He also became one of the famous personalities who suffered from learning disability although it didn't stop him from doing his responsibilities as a political leader in Great Britain during his time.

At 12-years-old, **George Patton** found he couldn't read. He remained deficient in reading all his life. However, he could memorize entire lectures, which was how he got through school. He became a famous general during WW II.

Dyslexia Military/Political: Royalty (Belgium)-Princess Tamara of Belgium; **Royalty (British)**-Prince Harry

#7 Presidents

Research shows that some past presidents are dyslexic or have ADHD characteristics. Most people have no clue as to what ADHD is, so it's likely that most wouldn't recognize someone with it.

Some media outlets describe President Donald Trump as abusing his power, ignorant and a pathological liar, impulsive, interrupting others, difficulty waiting his turn, blurting out answers, or having outbursts. (CNN Thinks Donald Trump Has Attention Deficit Disorder 2017) Could many of his behaviors be found in individuals who have ADHD?

My intent is to show the behaviors we witness daily on television that could point to ADHD characteristics. ADHD is when an individual has difficulty paying attention to the task at hand because of his or her inattentiveness, distraction, hyperactivity, or impulsivity.

Let's examine some of the situations that could point to characteristics of ADHD that President Trump has displayed. News shows and newspaper articles describe Trump's behaviors as being impulsive; a poor speller; and someone who blurts out tweets without thinking on Twitter. These few tidbits are just a fraction of the daily buzz found in the thousands of media stories, tweets, Facebook posts, etc.

One notable illustration of ADHD-type behavior such as impulsivity, frequent interruptions and blurting out answers during the presidential debate with Hillary Clinton. During the first debate, Trump interrupted Mrs. Clinton 55 times, while ignoring moderator Lester Holt's attempts to impose order. (Wilson 2016) Trump did much better in the second debate. However, he went back to his typical behavior of interruptions during the third and final debates. In fact, Trump interrupted Clinton and moderator Chris Wallace 48 times. (Johnson and Wilson 2016)

Researchers such as C. Keith Connors, professor emeritus of medical psychology at Duke University and creator of the Connors Rating Scales for diagnosing ADHD, says he always offers the same challenge: "Take one of these kids on a car trip for a day and see how you feel about it then." (Foley 2018) I concur 200% with Connors. The behaviors of ADHD are real. I've worked with ADHD students for more than 30 years, read countless books, and consulted with medical professionals and other experts on the topic. I am a Licensed Dyslexia Therapist (LDT) and a Certified Academic Language Therapist (CALT). I understand firsthand this type of disorder.

Many people with ADHD have ended up being successful business owners as you will notice in this chapter, which list individuals with disabilities.

Some of the biggest names in politics, in addition to sports, business, movie, and entertainment, have made significant contributions to our country despite their learning disabilities or ADHD. Through this book, it's our primary objective to aid in raising awareness about ADHD and other learning disorders.

"They misunderestimated me." It's been reported that former President **George W. Bush** has dyslexia. According to *Vanity Fair* magazine, he has problems with pronouncing words and using them in a sentence structure. (UnNews: Bush admits to being dyslexic 2008)

"Pessimism never won any battle." **Dwight D. "Ike" Eisenhower**, a five-star general, supreme commander of the Allied Forces in Europe, president of Columbia University, and the 34th U.S. president from 1953–1960 is believed to have had a learning disability. Most believe that Ike had some form of dyslexia.

"Determine never to be idle. No person will have occasion to complain of the want of time who never loses any. It is wonderful how much ay be done if we are always doing." It's believed that **Thomas Jefferson** battled several learning disabilities, such as stuttering and dyslexia. Jefferson, however, loved to read—his personal library contained thousands of books. He's remembered for authoring the Declaration of Independence, becoming the third U.S. president, and founding the University of Virginia.

"Only those who dare to fail greatly can ever achieve greatly." Despite having some form of dyslexia and chronic back pain, **John Fitzgerald Kennedy** attended Harvard and served in the Navy during World War II where he was awarded the Purple Heart and the World War II Victory Medal. JFK also served in both the House of Representatives and the Senate before becoming the 35th U.S president in 1960.

"What Washington needs is adult supervision." According to the *National Cynic*, after our 44th President Barrack Obama's first routine medical exam, White House physician, Jeffrey Kuhlman, found that the 48-year-old was in excellent health and fit for duty. What Kuhlman didn't divulge was that the president had been experiencing frequent headaches and dizziness. Like the test, the results, which showed a final diagnosis of "moderate dyslexia and mild ADD", also to remained secret.

"99% of failures come from people who make excuses." Throughout his life, **George Washington** struggled with spelling and grammar. It's widely believed that he had a learning disability, specifically dyslexia, and that he taught himself to correct the problem. Despite this learning disability, Washington became the father of our country after being the commander-in-chief of the Continental Army during the American Revolutionary War. He was elected unanimously as the first U.S. president.

"The man who is swimming against the stream knows the strength of it." **Woodrow Wilson** was not only a poor student; he could barely read by the age of 10. Thanks to his father who helped him overcome his severe form of dyslexia by teaching him the art of debate, Wilson went on to study law at the University of Virginia, became the president of Princeton University, and eventually 28th U.S. president from 1913–1921. Despite suffering a stroke while in office that left him partially paralyzed, Wilson was awarded Noble Peace Prize in 1919.

#8 Sports Figures and Athletes

Many of today's kids idolize professional athletes. They spend many hours watching these stars score, leap, dive, and tackle their way to Super Bowl titles, Olympic gold medals, Heisman Trophies, and World Series titles. What they don't see are the numerous years of hard work these athletes have spent to achieve their goals—The hours spent practicing; the sweat, tears, and sacrifices; failing, and falling down, and getting back up again.

Many athletes have also struggled in school for years due to learning disabilities. Learning disabilities are not handicaps; rather, having a learning disability simply means that some don't learn in typical ways. Their brains work differently so they learn differently.

Listed by their respective sport, here are some professional athletes who have struggled with learning disabilities:

Baseball: Before he was diagnosed, and subsequently treated, Major League Baseball pitcher **Scott Eyre** would get distracted after a conversation and not remember any of it. Eventually a team therapist pulled the southpaw pitcher aside and suggested he might have ADHD.

Basketball: A former LA Lakers professional basketball player, **Magic Johnson** has dyslexia and ADD. Magic added magic to all his games, resulting in a huge fan following to date even though he voluntary retired in 1991 after he received a shattering HIV diagnosis. Magic believes that everyone is special in their own unique ways and according to basketball-plays-and-tips.com once said, "You don't have to be Magic to special. You're already special, you're you".

Magic Johnson is also dyslexic, a disability that made it hard for him to perform well at school. "… the looks, the stares, the giggles … I wanted to show everybody that I could do better and also that I could read."

A professional basketball player, **Brandon Knight** has visual/special processing issues. Brandon was a straight-A student in high school and at the University of Kentucky, and some feel that his verbal/linguistic processing skills have improved since his school days. Knight holds a low career assist percentage (23%) and high turnover rate (15.6%) due to bad passes relative to other point guards. At Kentucky, John Calipari and other his coaches regularly reminded Knight to pass and share the ball with teammates.

Boxing: Widely regarded as one of the most significant and celebrated sports figures of the twentieth century, **Muhammad Ali**, an American boxer, grew up in Louisville, Kentucky, being called dumb due to his inability to read and his undiagnosed dyslexia. ⟩

Football: Former Pittsburgh Steelers quarterback and football analyst **Terry Bradshaw** revealed in his book Keep It Simple that he has struggled with ADHD for years.

Former NFL quarterback **Tim Tebow** has dyslexia. His father and brother do, too. Learning issues can run in families. He was diagnosed in elementary school and found ways to work around his reading difficulties. Tebow is one of many NFL players who have been open about their learning and attention issues. "It has to do with finding out how you learn," he said. "I'm not somebody that opens a playbook and just turns and reads and reads. So I just made flashcards. I take each one, and then boom, when I'm traveling, l just flip through it. That really helped me. Writing it down, flipping through and quizzing myself, that was a great way for me to do it."

Gymnastics: Simone Biles said ADHD is "nothing to be ashamed of." Biles disclosed her ADHD condition after her medical records were leaked by hackers. Approximately one month after, she took the Rio Olympics by storm on her way to four gold medals. "I have ADHD, and I have taken medicine for it since I was a kid. Please know, I believe in clean sport, have always followed the rules, and will continue to do so as fair play is critical to sport and is very important to me," said Biles. "Simone has filed the proper paperwork per USDA and WADA requirements, and there is no violation," Steve Perry, president of USA Gymnastics, said in a statement. "The International Gymnastics Federation, the United States Olympic Committee and USADA have confirmed this. Biles and everyone at USA Gymnastics believe in the importance of a level playing field for all athletes." While no one should be forced to discuss their medical history as a result of anonymous hackers, Biles made clear she isn't embarrassed to speak about her ADHD.

Skier: Anne Bancroft was the first woman to ski across Greenland and reach the North Pole by dogsled, polar explorer. Bancroft has long struggled with dyslexia.

Swimming: Michael Phelps holds the record for winning the most Olympic medals in swimming. He has ADHD and was hyperactive as a child. "I was always the kid that was running around," he said. "I literally could not sit still," His mother used his love of swimming to help him focus.

Track and Field: Michelle Carter, the 2016 Olympic gold medal winner, grew up with dyslexia and ADHD. Reading and spelling was, and still is, always a challenge for her. Williams says it was difficult to pay attention in school. But then she found her passion and talent in track and field. It motivated her to do well enough in school to be able to continue competing. It took her all the way to Rio in 2016, where she won an Olympic gold medal in shot put.

Caitlyn Jenner: Formerly known as Bruce Jenner, Caitlyn, wasn't always the reality star television dad we now know him as on "Keeping up with the Kardashians." Jenner was first an Olympic athlete in the arena of track and field. Jenner's struggle with dyslexia is actually what led him to sports and a new calling. In the 1976 Olympics, Jenner broke the world record for the decathlon and was handed an American flag. Taking his victory lap with it, Jenner's image was and continues to be seen across the world.

Dyslexia Sports: Baseball-Nolan Ryan; **Football**-Dexter Manley; **Sports Exec/Wrestling**-Vince McMahon; **Swimmer (Olympian)**-Greg Louganis; **Track and Field**-Bruce Jenner; **ADHD Sports: Baseball**-Scott Eyre, Pete Rose, Babe Ruth; **Race Car Driver**-Dusty Davis; **Track and Field (Olympian Runner)**-Carl Lewis (**ADHD/Dyslexia**),

Source List

Comprehensive source list for the list of celebrities, entertainers, entrepreneurs, leaders, military/political, presidents, and sports figures are lon the next pages.

Source #1 (50 Famously Successful People Who Are Dyslexic 2018): Ludweig Beethoven, Orlando Bloom, George Burns, Hans Christian Anderson, Agatha Christie, Tom Cruise, Leonardo Da Vinci, Walt Disney, Thomas Edison, F. Scott Fitzgerald, Tracey Gold, Alexander Graham Bell, Catilyn "Bruce" Jenner, John Lennon, Edward Olmos, George Patton, Pablo Picasso, Keanu Reeves, Lindsay Wagner, Robin Williams, Henry Winkler

Source #2 (Famous People With Dyslexia 2015): Will Smith

Source #3 (Bourgase 2014): Magic Johnson, Brandon Knight

Source #4 (List of Famous People with Learning Disabilities 2018): Albert Einstein, Danny Glover, Sylvester Stallone

Source #5 (Famous People With Dyslexia 2017): Tommy Hilfiger, Bruce Jenner, Kendall Jenner, Jay Leno, Paul Orfalea, Nolan Ryan, Vince Vaughn, John Chambers

Source #6 (Jonathan Ive – Dyslexic Genius 2017): Jonathan Ive

Source #7 (Tomcruiseversusarnoldschwarzenegger - Famous People With Learning Difficulties n.d.): David Bailey, Jim Carrey, Winston Churchill, Johnny Depp, Harrison Ford, Benjamin Franklin, Woody Harrelson, Prince Harry, Paris Hilton, Anthony Hopkins, Eddie Izzard, , Michael Jordan, Evel Kinevel , Carl Lewis, Lindsey Lohan, Greg Louganis, Dexter Manley, Vince McMahon, Mozart , Marilyn Monroe, Mary Tyler Moore, Jack Nicholson, Mary -Kate Olsen, Edger Allan Poe, Pete Rose, Socrates , Britney Spears, Princess Tamara of Belgium

Source #8 (Shoot 2018): Anne Bancroft, Terry Bradshaw, Erin Brockovich-Ellis, James Carville, Katherine Ellison, Ari Emanuel, Scott Eyre, Whoopi Goldberg, Salma Hayek, Howie Mandel, Phillip Manuel, Patrick McKenna, Alan Meckler, Roxy Olin, Jamie Oliver, Ty Pennington, Michael Phelps, Karina Smirnoff, Justin Timberlake

Source #9 (Rampton 2015): Dwight Eisenhower, Thomas Jefferson, John F. Kennedy, George Washington, Woodrow Wilson

Source #10 (Wright, Musicians With Learning and Attention Issues 2014-2018): Toni Bennett, Solange Knowles, Adam Levine, Ozzy Ozzbourne, Chris Robinson, Carla Simone

Source #11 (Athletes With Learning and Attention Issues. n.d.): Simone Biles, Michelle Carter, Dusty Davis

Source #12 (Game-Changers in History Who May Have Had Learning and Attention Issues 2014-2018): Harry Belafonte, Babe Ruth

Source #13 (Wright, Thanks, Mom: Quotes From Celebrities With Learning and Attention Issues 2014-2018): Muhammad Ali, Barbara Corcoran, Ryan Goslin, Daymond John, Trudie Styler, Channing Tatum, Florence Welch

Source #14 (Morin, Success Stories: Celebrities With Dyslexia, ADHD and Dyscalculia 2014-2018): David Boies, Cher, Anderson Cooper, Keira Knightley, Lisa Ling, Steven Spielberg, Tim Tebow

Chapter 9

How Sammy Can Learn to Read—A Service Delivery Plan

The National Crisis Continues

National statistics show that academic failure is rampant, especially in reading. In 2017, some 68 percent of 4th-grade students performed at or above the Basic achievement level in reading, according to NAEP. However, almost 4 out of 10 these fourth-graders struggle with basic reading skills and that most don't catch up without intensive intervention. Many of these students will never reach a level of reading proficiency that enables them to function in school, causing 10 to 15 percent to drop out of high school eventually. (McFarland, et al. 2018) Forty-four million adults—22 percent of the population—have limited reading skills. (Final Adult Basic Education Fact Sheet Updated 2017)

This crisis is unusually severe for the at-risk population. Research indicates that students who are at risk due to poverty, race, ethnicity, language, or other factors are rarely well-served by their local districts. In fact, they often attend schools where they are tracked into substandard courses and programs holding low expectations for learning. In the National Center for Education Statistics' *The Conditions of Education 2018* report, the data suggest that the long-term implications of negative tracking shows that graduation rates for such students are generally 15 to 20-percentage points lower than the national average.

The social costs of reading failure are also well-known. Surveys of adolescents and young adults with criminal records illustrate that about half have reading difficulties. Similarly, about half of youths with a history of substance abuse also have reading problems. Correctional officials say that 90 percent of all inmates are school dropouts, and 85 percent of those same inmates are functionally illiterate or can't read well. (The Economic & Social Cost of Illiteracy 2015)

The truth is that all children can learn when challenged by high expectations, rigorous academic standards, and proven programs. Most reading failure is due to undiagnosed learning disabilities (LD) or joint issues, such as ADHD, that impact a student's ability to learn. LD affect the way students of average-to-above-average intelligence receive and process specific information. It impacts their abilities to learn the basic skills of reading, writing, and math.

Triple A Educational Services, Inc.— "Focusing On Children in Underserved Communities"

Twenty-five years ago, I was concerned about the high illiteracy and drop-out rate in the African-American community. My vision was clarified when I witnessed my brother, Sam, struggle through school due to his undiagnosed dyslexia. Today, I want to keep other children from having this same painful experience. After studying a specialized reading program, I joined the advocacy efforts by creating a 501 (c) (3) nonprofit organization named FOCUS Centre of Learning, Inc., which was dedicated to serving children and adults with dyslexia, learning disabilities, and attention-deficit hyperactivity disorder (ADHD), and those individuals at-risk of failure because they can't read.

In 2017, a new vision to revise our organization was set into motion with renaming the organization to Triple A Educational Services, Inc. (TAES). This organization is dedicated to providing educational services to students who are at-risk of failure because they can't read or have learning disabilities that interfere with the normal learning process.

At TAES, we know that learning disabilities are neurological and that the earlier children are treated, the better chance they have to reach their potential. We test children as early as kindergarten to determine if they have reading challenges or other learning disabilities and train teachers and other degreed professionals to provide specialized programs.

TAES has a team of experts with a combined knowledge of more than 30 years of experience in teaching struggling readers and guiding teacher and/ or administrators through establishing and maintaining programs that can be integrated within schools or a small group.

The program at TAES is designed to especially educate minority communities about early diagnosis and remediation programs with an emphasis on specialized reading as a solution to cut illiteracy and lower the high crime rate. TAES is on a crusade to educate parents, teachers, and administrators on how to accurately identify and assess failing students who exhibit characteristics of dyslexia, LD, and ADHD. Our programs target children who cannot afford tuition for private school or tutoring programs, and who are likely to fall behind in public or private school system without specialized training. Our goal is to help return all educational school systems to a child-centered educational structure.

TAES is able to work with public, private, and charter schools by offering practical steps and assistance of service delivery models, which are specific strategy-driven techniques without placing a burden on a school's staff or budget. With a multisensory teaching model, schools are reenergized and prepared to transform their school into a culture of reading, restoring a student's reading confidence and improving a child's test scores.

Our cadre of services include the following:

1. **Curriculum for Reading.** Our curriculum utilizes research-based reading programs that recognize the nature of dyslexia and related language learning disabilities and the role of multisensory language instruction. Another hallmark of the program is the emphasis on reading remediation as the foundation of all other skills. We utilize the alphabetic phonics, now called Language Science, which is a structured language curriculum that implements multisensory teaching techniques through a discovery learning process. In the Language Science program, we use a structured and sequential structured phonics and phonological awareness program during and after-school in public, private, and charter schools.

2. **Teacher Training.** Our teacher-training program, named the Triple A Teacher Training Program, trains teachers to become Certified Academic Language Therapist (CALTs), Licensed Dyslexia Therapists, or practitioners, so they can learn and apply understandings about language and literacy to more effective instruction for at-risk students. Primary to our vision is continual specialized professional development. Our goal is to train 1,000 teachers in our graduate-level Teacher Training Program to provide instruction in multisensory teaching techniques. Upon course completion; which includes two years of training, hundreds of practice hours, observations, and a certification exam; at least 90 percent of these teachers will be eligible to apply for professional certification, and in some states, become a CALT as well as a Licensed Dyslexia Therapist.

3. **Interventions.** In the Language Science program, we use a structured and sequential phonics and phonological awareness program during and after school. TAES specializes in a service delivery model for the following school types:

- The whole school: Focusing primarily on heavily populated minority students who struggle with reading
- A small group: Focusing on dyslexic or LD students in need of differentiated instruction based on their progress in each of the language or literacy areas (that is, phoneme awareness, decoding, handwriting, and oral language)
- Summer school program: Establishes a four to a six-week program designed for undiagnosed or diagnosed dyslexic and LD students who perform below grade level in reading, writing, and math

4. **Professional Development/Workshops:** Effectively develop workshops, events, and professional development to gain interest from parents, teachers, administrators, and/or a school or organization's governance board. Our organization provides workshops, book studies, trainings, and events about increasing the awareness about dyslexia and learning disabilities for parents as well as professional development for teachers, administrators, and other professionals.

Carrying Forward a New Vision

The educational importance of being unable to read well can't be overstated. Like Sammy, the difficulty is painfully apparent when struggling readers try to read out loud. They stop and frequently start, mispronouncing some words, and skipping others entirely. The first casualty is self-esteem: Young children soon grow ashamed as they struggle with a skill that many of their classmates master easily. In later grades when children switch from learning-to-read to reading-to-learn, reading-impaired children are unable to explore science, history, literature, mathematics, and the wealth of information that is presented in print.

Beginning, struggling, or on-grade-level readers need practical skills to cope with the increasing demands of the rigor of local, state, and national tests to graduate from high school and matriculate into college or the working world. Schools are in a slump when it comes to offering simple, not to mention, specialized programs especially for nonreaders who are not on grade level due to an undiagnosed or diagnosed learning challenge, low-socio-economic conditions, and/or behavior.

Dyslexia accounts for 80 percent of all learning disabilities. (How many people are affected/at risk for learning disabilities? 2016)The importance of reading in a student's progress and emotional well-being is essential. Our specialized reading program covers three areas—a multisensory-structured language education and Orton-Gillingham curricula, an in-school intervention program using a multisensory-structured language to both regular and special education students, and the Triple A Teacher Training Program.

The next generation of programs and service at TAES is a model that the country can and should adopt to teach and prepare children for success while respecting their academic differences. TAES works with school governance, leadership, and staff to develop, implement, and monitor programs and their establishment and oversight of a detailed action plan for any service delivery model.

A Sustained Vision

Unfortunately, the demands from laws written by state lawmakers don't welcome or consider at-risk students with learning disabilities. The financial constraints, emphasis on high test results, and laws designed to decrease the number of charter schools crippled FOCUS's ability to continue serving LD students with in-school programs. Both of our charter schools have closed after 20-plus years of working with children.

Using our experience from FOCUS's private sessions, community outreach, and the charter schools, our new vision embodies a broader emphasis on helping all schools to expand their services to serve children with learning disabilities and others at risk.

In our efforts to continue reaching this at-risk population, our organization has taken a long-term view of student achievement. Instead of employing quick-fix programs that don't touch the heart of academic problems, we use strategies and programs emphasizing what is best educationally for LD children and give professionals, especially teachers, more specialized training in every classroom. We began our efforts in the highly populated minority schools in southern Dallas. There, we consolidated and targeted discretionary funding to implement a specific one-hour program for strengthening the capacity of those schools to effectively serve children with disabilities, including toddlers as young as four years old when appropriate.

The best strategy for preventing and correcting reading disabilities is explicit, systematic instruction guided by on-going assessment, which includes:

- Early support of letter knowledge and phonemic awareness
- Instruction on letter-sound correspondence and spelling conventions

- Opportunity and encouragement in using spelling-sound knowledge in reading and writing
- Daily sessions for independent and supported reading with attention on both fluency and comprehension
- Active exploration of new language, concepts, and modes of thought that are offered by written text

Creating a culture of reading is not easy. However, simple solutions do exist that require the willingness of teacher, administrators, and school governance to develop and implement researched-based interventions, provide teacher training, creatively adjust the school's schedule, and buy student materials.

Putting First Things First

One in six children who are not reading proficiently in 3rd grade fail to graduate from high school on time—four times the rate for children with proficient 3rd grade reading skills. (Hernandez 2011)

An effective and structured reading program designed to assist the struggling reader and/or a diagnosed LD student begins with a comprehensive action plan. Interested schools and organizations should identify key steps to improve the education of students starting in kindergarten. According to research from the Association for Supervision and Curriculum Development (ASCD), the essential components of an effective literacy action plan include implementation across the content; interventions for struggling readers; supportive school policies, procedures, and culture; leadership building; and teacher support.

TAES provides support, training, guidance, and technical assistance to schools wishing to adopt our Triple A Multi-Sensory Education (TAME) Program. With modification from TAES' team of experts, steps can be developed to jumpstart any school or organization's multi-sensory reading program to help struggling readers. The framework for this program consists of the TAME Overview and Action Plan, which is covered next. Teachers, administrators, and/or parents can adapt this program for their organization and present it to its governing board for consideration and approval in less than 30 days. This framework, which is discussed next, includes the steps to implement a multisensory education program in any school or an organization.

Steps to Start a Multisensory Education Program

Steps and Explanations:

1. Setting up an Action Team
    - Create a Triple A Multisensory Education Leadership Team to manage and prioritize the work and determine where resources are needed first.
2. Continue the practice of engaging teachers, administrators, and parents, to develop/refine the recommendations and implement strategies.
3. Determining your Goals and Objectives

Sample Goals:

- Have 150 students in grades first through third grade master the three-year intensive program, covering 85 percent of the English language
- Enable 150 students to read at or above their grade levels by the end of the three-year program
- Provide teachers with an opportunity to become Certified Academic Language Therapists (CALTs) to teach a specialized multisensory reading program

Objectives:

- Increase each participant's attendance to 85 percent.
- Have students complete one schedule in first grade and two schedules in second and third grades by the end of the program's first year.
- Have students complete two schedules in first grade and three schedules for second and third grades by the end of the program's second year.
- Have students complete three to four schedules in first grade and four to five schedules for second and third grades by the end of the program's third year.
- Train and monitor staff for three years in using an innovative reading approach to teach students how to read and pass state-required standardized tests.
- Have 20 teachers certified as Certified Academic Language Therapists (CALTs) by the end of the program's third year.

4. Conducting a Needs Assessment

The Triple A Multisensory Education Leadership Team will conduct a needs assessment by collecting, reviewing, and summarizing student performance data.

5. Creating a school capacity profile

The team will outline what capacities, structures, and policies need to be put into place. The team should be well on its way to understanding the assets the school already has to contribute to the reading effort. Support of the school's reading program involves time, personnel, scheduling, and a suitable location.

School structures that support reading are as follows:

- Additional strategic reading classes or reading workshops
- Daily morning reading relevant to the day's work
- Portfolio assessment and student exhibitions
- Scheduled reading times that are school-wide or for small groups at least 3 to 5 times weekly
- Quarterly joint team meetings

School resources and policy that support reading are as follows:

- Properly set up classrooms
- Reading programs for learners with targeted reading needs
- Technology-supported reading instruction and assessment
- Curriculum materials of varying reading levels for study
- Specialized reading coach positions
- Professional teacher development
- Regularly scheduled student reading assessments as part of the educational experience

6. Creating and Adopting the Triple A Multi-Sensory Education Program Proposal

Your leadership team can create a TAME Program proposal using the sample model found in Appendix A.

- Your leadership team should submit its TAME Program Overview and Action Plan to the school or organization's governance for consideration and approval. A sample overview and action plan listed in the Appendix A.

References

n.d. Accessed July 12, 2018. https://www.merriam-webster.com/.

2017. "2017 World Population Data Sheet-Population Reference Bureau." *PRB.org.* Accessed August 12, 2018. https://www.prb.org/wp-content/uploads/2017/08/2017_World_Population.pdf.

n.d. *22 Dyslexic Billionaires.* Accessed July 26, 2017. https://dyslexia.com.au/dyslexic-billionaires/.

n.d. *25 Famous People with Learning Disorders.* Accessed July 25, 2017. http://www.special-education-degree.net/25-famous-people-with-learning-disorders/.

2017. "39th Annual Report to Congress on the Implementation of the Individuals with Disabilities Education Act, 2017." Annual, Office of Special Education and Rehabilitative Services, Office of Special Education Programs, U.S. Department of Education,, Washington, DC. Accessed August 16, 2018. https://www2.ed.gov/about/reports/annual/osep/2017/parts-b-c/39th-arc-for-idea.pdf.

2018. *50 Famously Successful People Who Are Dyslexic.* Accessed September 20, 2018. http://www.psychologydegree.com/50-famously-successful-people-who-are-dyslexic.

2018. *Abigail Adams Quotes II: American First Lady (1744-1818).* Accessed August 28, 2018. http://www.notable-quotes.com/a/adams_abigail_ii.html.

2015. "ADHD Information Packet." *Support for Families of Children with Disabilities.* Center for Parent Center for Parent Information and Resources. February. Accessed August 16, 2018. www.supportforfamilies.org.

2011. "ADHD: Clinical Practice Guideline for the Diagnosis, Evaluation, and Treatment of Attention-Deficit/Hyperactivity Disorder in Children and Adolescents." *American Academy of Pediatrics* 128 (5). Accessed August 29, 2018. http://pediatrics.aappublications.org/content/128/5/1007.

2002. "Annual Statistical Report Public Schools of Arkansas and Educational Service Cooperatives." Arkansas Department of Education. Accessed September 9, 2018. http://www.arkansased.gov/public/userfiles/Fiscal_and_Admin_Services/Publication%20and%20reports/ASR/ASR_01-02.pdf.

The Understood Team, ed. n.d. *Athletes With Learning and Attention Issues.* Accessed July 25, 2017. https://www.understood.org/en/learning-attention-issues/personal-stories/famous-people/athletes-with-learning-and-attention-issues.

n.d. *Attention Deficit Hyperactivity Disorder (ADHD).* Accessed June 20, 2017. https://www.ncbi.nlm.nih.gov/pubmedhealth/PMHT0024867/.

2018. *Attention-Deficit/Hyperactivity Disorder (ADHD).* March 20. Accessed August 26, 2018. https://www.cdc.gov/ncbddd/adhd/facts.html.

2016. "Attention-Deficit/Hyperactivity Disorder (ADHD): The Basics." Vers. Revised. *Nimh.Nih.Gov.* Accessed July 24, 2018. https://www.nimh.nih.gov/health/publications/attention-deficit-hyperactivity-disorder-adhd-the-basics/index.shtml.

n.d. *Auditory Processing Disorder.* Accessed July 13, 2018. https://ldaamerica.org/types-of-learning-disabilities/auditory-processing-disord.

Barkley, R. 2008. "Classroom Accommodations for Children with ADHD." *The ADHD Report* (The ADHD Report). Accessed August 29, 2018. http://www.russellbarkley.org/factsheets/ADHD_School_Accommodations.pdf.

Barkley, R. 2017. "What Causes ADHD?" *Gilford.* Accessed August 28, 2018. www.russellbarkley.org/factsheets/WhatCausesADHD2017.pdf.

Barth, J., and K. A. Nitta. 2008. "Education in the Post-Lake View Era: What is Arkansas Doing To Close the Achievement Gap?" Accessed September 9, 2018. https://static1.squarespace.com/static/55afb880e4b039b081c51cbc/t/55ba3abce4b01ce0dc198a16/1438371752817/Achievement+Gap+2008+Full+copy.pdf.

Basch, C. 2011. "Inattention and Hyperactivity and the Achievement Gap Among Urban Minority Youth." *Journal of School Health* 81 (10): 641-649. Accessed July 30, 2018. http://www.rmc.org/wpdev/wp-content/uploads/2012/12/Inattention-   and-Hyperactivity-and-the-Achievement-Gap-Among-Urban-Minority-Youth.pdf.

Bates, M. 2013-2018. *Orton Gillingham Instructional Approach Orton Gillingham Quick Facts.* Accessed August 28, 2018. https://www.dyslexia-reading-well.com/orton-gillingham.html.

2016. "Behavior Therapy for Children with ADHD: An Overview." *CDC.gov.* National Center on Birth Defects and Developmental Disabilities. Accessed August 29, 2018. https://www.cdc.gov/ncbddd/adhd/documents/adhd-behavior-therapy-overview-all-ages.pdf.

Berninger, V., and T. Richards. 2015. *Research confirms what many teachers know: Learning Disabilities is a plural word.* October. Accessed May 22, 2018. https://dyslexiaida.org/research-confirms-what-many-teachers-know-learning-disabilities-are-plural/.

Black, Albert, interview by L. McClure, Jr. 2017. *Interview with Albert Black* Dallas, Texas, (April).

Bourgase, B. 2014. *Sport and Learning Disabilities.* July. Accessed August 14, 2017. http://www.bourgase.com/teaching/special-education/sport-and-learning-disabilities/.

2017. *Census Bureau Projects U.S. and World Populations on New Year's Day.* Vers. RELEASE NUMBER CB17-TPS.88. December 28. Accessed August 13, 2018. https://www.census.gov/newsroom/press-releases/2017/new-years-2018.html.

Chingos, M. M. 2015. "Breaking the Curve: Promises and Pitfalls of Using NAEP Data to Assess the State Role in Student Achievement." Vers. Updated. October.

Accessed May 22, 2018. https://www.urban.org/research/publication/breaking-curve-promises-and-pitfalls-using-naep-data-assess-state-role-student-achievement.

Clark, L. 2014. *30 Different Types of Doctors and What They Do.* April 14. Accessed July 24, 2018. https://blog.udemy.com/different-types-of-doctors/.

2017. *CNN Thinks Donald Trump Has 'Attention Deficit Disorder.* January 28. Accessed June 19, 2017. https://pjmedia.com/video/cnn-thinks-donald-trump-has-attention-deficit-disorder/.

Cortiella, C., and S. H. Horowitz. 2014. "The State of Learning Disabilities: Facts, Trends and Emerging Issues." New York: National Center for Learning Disabilities, New York. Accessed May 22, 2018. https://www.ncld.org/wp-content/uploads/2014/11/2014-State-of-LD.pdf.

ATTITUDE, ed. 2017. *Could Donald Trump Have ADHD?* July. Accessed July 18, 2018. https://www.additudemag.com/does-donald-trump-have-adhd/.

n.d. *Definitions.* Accessed July 25, 2017. https://www.dictionary.com/browse/remediation.

2013. *Diagnostic and Statistical Manual of Mental Disorders.* Fifth Edition: DSM-5. Washington: American Psychiatric Association.

n.d. *Different Types of Doctors & Medical Specialists Explained.* Accessed July 24, 2018. https://www.webmd.com/health-insurance/insurance-doctor-types?print=true.

Dragoo, K. E. 2017. "The Individuals with Disabilities Education Act (IDEA), Part B: Key Statutory and Regulatory Provisions." June 14. Accessed May 22, 2018. https://fas.org/sgp/crs/misc/R41833.pdf.

Dutton, J. 2006. *ADHD Athletes: Inspiring Sports Stars with Attention Deficit.* July. Accessed July 24, 2018. http://www.additudemag.com/adhd/article/989.html.

Esperian, J. H. 2010. "The Effect of Prison Education Programs on Recidivism." *Correctional Education Association* 61 (4): 316334. Accessed May 22, 2018. http://www.jstor.org/stable/23282764.

Estante, R. 2015. *An Interview with Dr. Julie Schweitzer – Part I.* September 20. Accessed July 20, 2018. https://add.org/an-interview-with-dr-julie-schweitzer-part-i-2/.

Evans, S. W., J. S. Owens, and N. Bunford. 2013. "Evidence-Based Psychosocial Treatments for Children and Adolescents with Attention-Deficit/Hyperactivity Disorder." *Journal of Clinical Child & Adolescent Psychology* 43 (4): 527-551. Accessed August 28, 2018. doi:10.1080/15374416.2013.850700 .

2018. *Fact Sheet: Disability and health.* January 16. Accessed September 18, 2018. http://www.who.int/en/news-room/fact-sheets/detail/disability-and-health .

2011. *Famous People with Dyslexia.* Accessed July 26, 2017. http://www.dyslexiaspeaks. com/html/famous.html.

2017. *Famous People With Dyslexia.* Accessed September 18, 2018. https://thepow-erofdyslexia.com/famous-dyslexics/.

2015. *Famous People With Dyslexia.* Accessed September 23, 2018. https://dyslexia.com.au/free-dyslexia-learning/famous-people-with-dyslexia/.

COABE, ed. 2017. "Final Adult Basic Education Fact Sheet Updated." *COABE.* Accessed September 15, 2018. https://static1.squarespace.com/static/55a158b4e4b0796a90 f7c371/t/58a0add09de4bbd20b9b7957/1486925280025/Adult%2BBasic% 2BEducation%2BFact%2BSheet+Updated.pdf.

Foley, D. 2018. *Growing Up with ADHD.* Accessed August 27, 2018. http://time.com/growing-up-with-adhd/.

The Understood Team, ed. 2014-2018. *Game-Changers in History Who May Have Had Learning and Attention Issues.* Accessed September 22, 2018. https://www.understood.org/en/learning-attention-issues/personal-stories/fa-mous-people/historical-figures-who-may-have-had-learning-and-attention-is-sues?view=slideview.

Garger, S. 2001. "Diversity, Learning Style and Culture." New Horizons for Learning, October. Accessed December 13, 2018. http://archive.education.jhu.edu/PD/ne-whorizons/strategies/topics/Learning%20Styles/diversity.html. 2018. *Glossary of Terms.* Accessed August 30, 2018. http://www.chadd.org/Understanding-ADHD/About-ADHD/Glossary-of-Terms.aspx.

Goode, D. 2018. "Navigating Learning Disabilities and the Cost for Treatment." Accessed August 30, 2018.

Hardoon, D. 2015. "Wealth: Having It All and Wanting More." *oxfam.org.* January 19. Accessed August 11, 2018. https://www.oxfam.org/en/research/wealth-hav-ing-it-all-and-wanting-more.

Hernandez, D. J. 2011. *Double Jeopardy: How Third Grade Reading Skills and Pov-erty Influence High School Graduation Rate.* Report-Research, University at Al-bany, State University of New York, Baltimore, MD: The Annie E. Casey Foun-dation. Accessed May 22, 2018. https://files.eric.ed.gov/fulltext/ED518818.pdf.

Honos-Webb, L. 2005. *The Gift of ADHD: how to transform your child's problems into strengths.* New Harbinger Publications, Inc.

Horowitz, S.H., J. Rawe, and M. C. Whittaker. 2017. "The State of Learning Disabil-ities: Understanding the 1 in 5." Report, National Center for Learning Disabili-ties, New York. Accessed May 22, 2018. https://www.ncld.org/about-this-report.

Horst, J. S. 2013. "Context and repetition in word learning." *Frontiers in Psychology* 4: 149. Accessed September 9, 2018. doi:10.3389/fpsyg.2013.00149.

2016. *How many people are affected/at risk for learning disabilities?* The Communi-cations Office. December 1. Accessed July 12, 2018. www.nichd.nih.gov/health/topics/learning/conditioninfo/risk.

Hunter, P. C. 2012. *It's Not Complicated: What I Know for Sure About Helping Our Students of Color Become Successful Readers.* New York: Scholastic Teaching Resources.

Johnson, D., and C. Wilson. 2016. *Donald Trump's 'Nasty Woman' Comment Was 1 of His 48 Interruptions at the Presidential Debate.* October 20. Accessed June 12, 2017. http://time.com/4538271/donald-trump-nasty-woman-interruption-presidential-debate.

2017. *Jonathan Ive – Dyslexic Genius.* Accessed September 23, 2018. https://thepowerofdyslexia.com/jonathan-ive-dyslexic-genius/ .

Lambek, R., R. Tannock, and S. Dalsgaardall. 2011. "Executive Dysfunction in School-Age Children With ADHD." *Journal of Attention Disorders* (NCBI) 15 (6): 646-655. Accessed September 8, 2018. doi:10.1177/10870547103709.

n.d. *Language Processing Disorder.* Accessed July 15, 2017. https://ldaamerica.org/types-of-learning-disabilities/language-processing-disorder/.

2012. *Laws & Guidance Civil Rights: Disability Discrimination.* https://www2.ed.gov/policy/rights/guid/ocr/disability.html. September 21. Accessed August 24, 2018. https://www2.ed.gov/policy/rights/guid/ocr/disability.html.

n.d. *Learning Disabilities Information Page.* Accessed July 15, 2017. https://www.ninds.nih.gov/disorders/all-disorders/learning-disabilities-information-page.

2013. *Learning Disorders No. 16.* August. Accessed July 24, 2018. https://www.aacap.org/AACAP/Families_and_Youth/Facts_for_Families/FFF-Guide/Children-With-Learning-Disorders-016.aspx.

Mayo Clinic Staff, ed. 2016. *Learning disorders: Know the signs, how to help.* February 10. Accessed July 21, 2018. https://www.mayoclinic.org/healthy-lifestyle/childrens-health/in-depth/learning-disorders/art-20046105.

Lerner, J. W. 2000. *Learning disabilities: Theories, diagnosis, and teaching strategies.* 8th.

Leviz, E. 2017. *All the Terrifying Things That Donald Trump Did Lately.* June 9. Accessed June 12, 2017. http://nymag.com/daily/intelligencer/2017/06/every-terrifying-thing-that-donald-trump-has-done.html.

1997. "Learning for All." By L. W. Lezotte, 92. Effective School Products.

2011. *Life Application Study Bible.* New International Version. Tyndale House Publishers. Accessed July 25, 2017.

2018. *List of Famous People with Learning Disabilities.* Accessed September 18, 2018. https://healthresearchfunding.org/list-famous-people-learning-disabilities/ .

Lonigan, C. L., and T. Shanahan. n.d. "Executive Summary | Developing Early Literacy: Report of The National Early Literacy Panel." Executive Summary, National Institute for Literacy. Accessed August 16, 2018. https://www1.nichd.nih.gov/publications/pubs/documents/NELPSummary.pdf.

Maxwell, J. C. 2014. "The 15 Invaluable Laws of Growth: Live Them and Reach Your Potential." 288. Center Street (Reprint edition).

McFarland, J., B. Hussar, X. Wang, A. Rathbun, E. F. Cataldi, and F. B. Mann. 2018. "The Condition of Education 2018 (NCES 2018-144)." McFarland, J., Hussar, B., Wang, X., Zhang, J., Wang, K., Rathbun, A., Barmer, A., Forrest Cataldi, E., and Bullock Mann, F., National Center for Education, U.S. Department of Education., Washington, DC. Accessed July 20, 2018. https://nces.ed.gov/pub-search/pubsinfo.asp?pubid=2018144.

2012. *Men Occasionally Stumble Over the Truth, But They Pick Themselves Up and Hurry Off.* May 26. https://quoteinvestigator.com/2012/05/26/stumble-over-truth/.

2002. *Miles to Go, Arkansas.* Study, Arkansas Advisory Council of Governors and Advisory Committee, Atlanta: Southern Education Foundation, SEF, 1-25. Accessed September 9, 2018. http://www.southerneducation.org/getattachment/9fdc0149-a5 48-4eaf-8db2-9fa0cefd8235/Miles-To-Go-Arkansas.aspx.

Moats, L. 2006. "How Spelling Supports Reading And Why It Is More Regular And Predictable Than You May Think." *American Federation of Teachers* (Winter 2005/06): 1-22, 42-43. Accessed September 6, 2018. https://www.aft.org/sites/default/files/periodicals/Moats.pdf .

Moats, L., and M. L. Farrell. 2005. *Multisensory Structured Language Education: Multisensory Teaching of Basic Language Skills.* Edited by Judith Birsh. Baltimore, MD: Paul H. Brookes Publishing.

Morin, A. 2015. "Learning Disabilities Information Packet." *Support for Families of Children with Disabilities.* Center for Parent Center for Parent Information and Resources. February. Accessed August 16, 2018. www.supportforfamilies.org .

—. 2014-2018. *Success Stories: Celebrities With Dyslexia, ADHD and Dyscalculia.* Accessed July 25, 2017. https://www.understood.org/en/learning-attention-is-sues/personal-stories/famous-people/success-stories-celebrities-with-dyslex-ia-adhd-and-dyscalculia.

—. 2014-2018. *Successful Entrepreneurs With Learning and Attention Issues.* Accessed September 22, 2018. https://www.understood.org/en/learning-attention-issues/personal-stories/famous-people/successful-entreprneurs-with-learning-and-attention-issues?view=slideview.

Morris, B., L. M. Resear, and P. Neering. 2002. *Overcoming Dyslexia.* May 13. Accessed September 25, 2018. http://archive.fortune.com/magazines/fortune/for-tune_archive/2002/05/13/322876/index.htm.

2018. "Multisensory teaching of basic language skills." Edited by J. Birsh and J. Car-reker. Baltimore, Maryland: Paul H. Brookes Publishing Company. Accessed September 7, 2018.

n.d. "NAEP in the National Conversation: Black Male Achievement, National Assessment of Educational Progress (NAEP)." Vers. last modified July 23, 2014.

nces.ed.gov. Accessed July 13, 2018. https://nces.ed.gov/nationsreportcard/blog/blogpost_brothers_keeper.aspx.

Narkon, D. E., and J. C. Wells. 2013. "Improving Reading Comprehension for Elementary Students with Learning Disabilities: UDL Enhanced Story Mapping." 57 (4). Accessed May 22, 2018. doi:10.1080/1045988X.2012.726286.

n.d. *Non-Verbal Learning Disabilities.* Accessed July 15, 2017. https://ldaamerica.org/types-of-learning-disabilities/non-verbal-learning-disabilities/.

2014. *Parent Tips LD online LD Basics.* September 26. Accessed August 16, 2018. http://www.ldonline.org/ldbasics/parenttips?theme=print.

Pastor, P. N., C. A. Reuben, C. R. Duran, and L. D. Hawkins. 2015. *Association Between Diagnosed ADHD and Selected Characteristics Among Children Aged 4–17 Years: United States, 2011–2013.* NCHS Data Brief, U.S. Department of Health and Human Services, Centers for Disease Control and Prevention, Hyattsville, MD: National Center for Health Statistics, 8. Accessed August 27, 2018. https://www.cdc.gov/nchs/data/databriefs/db201.pdf.

2017. "Psychosocial Treatment for Children & Adolescents with ADHD." *Children and Adults with Attention-Deficit/Hyperactivity Disorder (CHADD).* Accessed August 30, 2018. http://www.chadd.org/Portals/0/Content/CHADD/NRC/Factsheets/Psychosocial%20Treatments%20for%20Children%20with%20 20ADHD.pdf.

Rampton, J. 2015. "11 U.S. Presidents Who Overcame a Disability." *Inc.* August 25. Accessed August 14, 2017. https://www.inc.com/john-rampton//11-us-presidents-who-overcame-a-disability.html.

2015. *Research Confirms What Many Teachers Know: Learning Disabilities Are Plural.* October. Accessed July 24, 2018. https://dyslexiaida.org/research-confirms-what-many-teachers-know-learning-disabilities-are-plural/.

Reynolds, J. L. 2017. *A Child With ADHD Likely to Have Additional Behavioral Issues, Anxiety.* June 30. Accessed August 30, 2018. https://health.usnews.com/health-care/patient-advice/articles/2017-06-30/a-child-with-adhd-likely-to-have-additional-behavioral-issues-anxiety.

Ritter, G. W. 2002. "Education Reform in Arkansas: Past and Present." http://media.hoover.org/sites/default/files/documents/P0502_27.pdf.

Rosenzweig, K. 2009. "Are Today's General Education Teachers Prepared to Meet the Needs of Their Inclusive Students?" *NERA Conference Proceedings 2009.* 10. Accessed August 13, 2018. http://digitalcommons.uconn.edu/nera_2009/10.

Sachs, G. 2016. *Does Trump Have ADHD? My Professional Opinion.* Vers. Updated. August 18. Accessed June 19, 2017. http://m.huffpost.com/us/entry/1156800 2.

Sainato, M. 2017. *US Prison System Plagued by High Illiteracy Rates Inability to read traps inmates in the criminal justice system.* July 18. Accessed August 13, 2018. observer.com/2017/07/prison-illiteracy-criminal-justice-reform/.

Segal, J., and M. Smith. 2016. *Teaching Students with ADD/ADHD.* Accessed September 6, 2018. http://www.helpguide.org/articles/add-adhd/ teaching-students-with-adhd-attention-defi-.

Shapley, T. 2017. *Frederick Douglass Quotes on Slavery, Injustice, and Other Evil Things.* December 7. Accessed August 27, 2018. https://bookriot.com/2017/12/07/frederick-douglass-quotes.

Shaywitz, S. 2005. *Overcoming Dyslexia: A New and Complete Science-Based Program for Reading Problems at Any Level.* 1 edition. New York: Vintage.

Shear, M. D., and E. Huetterman. 2017. *Trump Repeats Lie About Popular Vote in Meeting with Lawmakers.* Vers. Last modified. January 23. Accessed June 25, 2017. https://www.nytimes.com/2017/01/23/us/politics/donald-trump-congress-democrats.html.

Sheehy, G. 2000. *The Presidency The Accidental Candidate.* October. Accessed July 25, 2017. https://www.vanityfair.com/news/2000/10/bush200010.

Shields, K. A., K. D. Cook, and S. Greller. 2016. "How kindergarten entry assessments are used in public schools and how they correlate with spring assessments." U.S. Department of Education, Institute of Education Sciences, National Center for Education Evaluation and Regional Assistance, Regional Educational Laboratory Northeast & Islands, Washington, D.C. Accessed August 27, 2018. http://ies.ed.gov/ncee/edlabs.

Shoot, B. 2018. *The Stars Who Aligned ADHD with Success.* Accessed September 15, 2018. https://www.additudemag.com/successful-people-with-adhd-learning-disabilities/.

1997. *Snapshot '97: 1996-97 School District Profiles.* Texas Education Agency. Accessed June 19, 2017. https://rptsvr1.tea.texas.gov/perfreport/snapshot/97/text/stuperf.html.

Stanovich, K. E. 1986. "Matthew effects in reading: Some consequences of individual differences in the acquisition of literacy." *Reading Research Quarterly* 21: 360-406.

Stuart, A. 2014. *Managing AD/HD with medication: An overview.* July 10. Accessed August 16, 2018. http://www.greatschools.org/print-view/special-education/LD-ADHD/735-managing-ADHD-with-medication.gs?fromPage=all.

Suits, S., K. Dunn, and N. Sabree. 2014. "Just Learnning The Imperative to Transform Juvenile Justice Systems Into Effective Educational Systems." A Study of Juvenile Justice Schools in the South and the Nation, Southern Education Foundation, Inc., Atlanta, 46. Accessed August 14, 2018. https://static.prisonpolicy.org/scans/Just-Learning-Final.pdf.

Sullivan, A. L., N. Kohli, E. M. Fainsworth, S. Sadeh, and L. Jones. 2017. "Longitudinal Models of Reading Achievement of Students with Learning Disabilities and without Disabilities." *School Psychology Quarterly* 32 (3): 336-349. doi:10.1037/spq0000170.

n.d. "Take Flight Program." Accessed July 12, 2018. amltherapy.com/wp-content/uploads/2012/01/Take_Flight_Program.pdf.

Tatum, S., and J. Acosta. 2017. *Report: Trump continues to question Obama's birth certificate.* November 29. Accessed August 27, 2018. https://www.cnn.com/2017/11/28/politics/donald-trump-barack-obama-birth-certificate-nyt/index.html.

2009. "Teach Them All to Read: Catching the Kids Who Fall Through the Cracks." Edited by E. K. McEwan-Adkins, 248. Thousand Oaks, CA: Corwin.

Texas Education Agency. 1999. "Grade 3 Classrooms and Student Performance in Texas Public Schools." STEPS Report 6A, Texas Education Agency, Austin, TX. https://tea.texas.gov/acctres/Spec_steps_6a_1999.pdf.

2007-2018. *Texas Essential Knowledge and Skills.* Accessed June 12, 2017. https://tea.texas.gov/curriculum/teks/.

2015. "The Economic & Social Cost of Illiteracy: A snapshot of illiteracy in a global context." Final report, World Literacy Foundation, 18. Accessed September 15, 2018. https://worldliteracyfoundation.org/wp.../WLF-FINAL-ECONOMIC-REPORT.pdf.

n.d. *The State of LD: Identifying Struggling Students.* Accessed July 25, 2017. https://www.ncld.org/identifying-struggling-students.

2018. *The State of LD: Understanding Learning and Attention Issues.* National Center for Learning Disabilities. Accessed July 14, 2018. https://www.ncld.org/understanding-learning-and-attention-issues.

2015. "The-Economic-Social-Cost-of-Illiteracy." *World Literacy Foundation.* Accessed September 15, 2018. https://worldliteracyfoundation.org/wp-content/uploads/2015/05/The-Economic -Social-Cost-of-Illiteracy.pdf.

2016. "Tips for Educators Helping Students with ADHD Using the Instructional Process." *Children and Adults with Attention-Deficit/Hyperactivity Disorder (CHADD).* Accessed September 5, 2018. www.chadd.org/nrc.

n.d. *Tomcruiseversusarnoldschwarzenegger - Famous People With Learning Difficulties.* Accessed June 26, 2017. https://tomcruiseversusarnoldschwarzenegger.weebly.com/.

2007. "Truth in Labeling: Disproportionality in Special Education ." National Education Association and National Association of School Psychologists . Accessed July 17, 2018. https://www.nea.org/assets/docs/HE/EW-TruthInLabeling.pdf.

Tucker, P., and J. Stronge. 2005. "Linking Teacher Evaluation and Student Learning." *Association for Supervision and Curriculum Development. (ASCD).* Accessed September 8, 2018. http://www.ascd.org/publications/books/104136/chapters/The-Power-of-an-Effective-Teacher-and-Why-We-Should-Assess-It.aspx.

n.d. *Types of Learning Disabilities.* Accessed July 15, 2017. https://ldaamerica.org/types-of-learning-disabilities/ Types of Learning Disabilities.

2014. "U.S. Departments of Education and Justice, Guiding Principles for Providing High-Quality Education in Juvenile Justice Secure Care Settings." Washington, D.C. Accessed July 30, 2018.

2008. *UnNews: Bush admits to being dyslexic.* November 16. Accessed July 25, 2017. http://uncyclopedia.wikia.com/wiki/UnNews:Bush_admits_to_being_dyslexic.

Vaughn, S, C Bos, and J. S. Schumm. 2007. *Teaching students who are exceptional, diverse, and at risk in the general education classroom.* 4th. New York: Pearson Education, Inc.

Wilson, C. 2016. *Donald Trump Interrupted Hillary Clinton and Lester Holt 55 Times in the First Presidential Debate.* September 27. Accessed June 12, 2017. http://time.com/4509790/donald-trump-debate-interruptions/.

Wolf, B., and V. Berninger. 2015. "Specific learning disabilities: Plural, definable, diagnosable, and treatable." International Dyslexia Association Newsletter for Parents Dyslexia Connections. March 20. Accessed July 24, 2018.

Wright, L. W. 2014-2018. *10 Oscar Winners With Dyslexia.* Accessed September 17, 2018. https://www.understood.org/en/learning-attention-issues/personal-stories/famous-people/10-oscar-winners-with-dyslexia?view=slideview.

—. 2014-2018. *Musicians With Learning and Attention Issues.* Accessed September 18, 2018. https://www.understood.org/en/learning-attention-issues/personal-stories/famous-people/.

—. 2014-2018. *Thanks, Mom: Quotes From Celebrities With Learning and Attention Issues.* Accessed September 17, 2018. https://www.understood.org/en/learning-attention-issues/personal-stories/famous-people/thanks-mom-quotes-from-celebrities-with-learning-and-attention-issues?view=slideview.

Appendices A

Sample Triple A Multi-Sensory Education Program (TAME) Overview

TAME Program Overview	
Service Delivery Model	**TAME Program:** This program can be tweaked for any public, private, or charter school to address reading deficits of students through multisensory techniques and Orton-Gillingham's Alphabetic Phonics (AP) Programs and strategies.
Goal	The goals are as follows: • Teachers will teach language science to 150 children during an in-school session for three years beginning in the start of the school year. • Sessions will be conducted by a trained Certified Academic Language Therapist (CALT) during regular school hours when children are most alert and so that he/she have time for after-school extracurricular activities and homework. • Each CALT will teach 500 sessions during each academic school year. • Sessions will be conducted Mondays through Thursdays. • Each session will be held one hour for a group consisting of 6 to 10 students.
Curriculum	This program is a complete multisensory phonics program designed for the undiagnosed or diagnosed dyslexic child and the child who can't read. It's built on a step-by-step approach using intensive phonics. Students use their auditory, visual, and kinesthetic senses as they interact in a one-hour Language Science class, also known as a language therapy session. The session's use of phonics covers ABCs, long- and short-vowel sounds, beginning and ending sounds, blends, clusters, digraphs, combinations, trigraphs, affixes, basic sight words, word attack skills, etc. These skills teach all children to read, not just the dyslexic or LD child. The AP curriculum consists of 11 multisensory activities. These two- to ten-minute activities take into consideration the short attention span of many students. The daily schedule of activities includes, but is not limited to: • *Language Study:* Students review the development of language as they're taught they can read, write, and spell 85 percent of standard English if they learn the code upon which it is based.

	• *Alphabetic Study:* Students study and practice the alphabet, which leads to learning dictionary skills.
	• *Reading Decks:* Students take part in reinforcement activities to identify and instantly name each grapheme and translate it into speech sounds.
	• *Instant Deck:* Students take part in reinforcement activities to learn how to instantly translate each speech sound into the spelling letter, which most often represents it.
	• *Multisensory Introduction of New Letters:* Letters and letter clusters are introduced to the students for reading, writing, and spelling through eight multisensory linkages.
	• *Reading Practice:* Students learn how to apply the code for accuracy, fluency, and comprehension.
	• *Handwriting Practice:* Cursive writing is used throughout the program as emphasis is placed on naming a letter before a student begins writing it.
	• *Spelling:* The student's application of sound-symbol relationships is supported and learned via practice of the Instant Spelling Deck.
	• *Verbal Support:* Organized oral expression is encouraged by students, in addition to the development of word pictures and expression transition into written expression.
	• *Review:* Brief reviews of the day's new discoveries and previously taught concepts occur daily.
	• *Listening:* High-interest selections are read by the teacher to increase listening and comprehension skills, as well as provide a daily treat.
Targeted Students	**Timely Identification:** The principal, teachers, and/or counselors are asked to recommend a pool of students who are considered to be at risk of failure in reading or illustrate symptoms of dyslexia or other learning disabilities. Suggested targeted students are those found in: • Kindergarten through third grades minimally, but can be found up to the fifth grade • The six to eighth grades where students can use the older version of the Language Science program

The Program Schedule	• A one-hour session held during the first hour of the school, called the Power Hour, from 8 a.m. to 9 a.m. *Suggestion:* Each teacher of kindergarten through third grade should use this to teach the language science curriculum. • The one-hour session is offered a minimum of four times daily to serve more students.
Occurrence Frequency	Four days a week (Mondays through Thursdays) during regular school hours
Session Guidelines	Language Science Session Guidelines are as follows: 1. To present all new material through visual, auditory, and kinesthetic channels 2. To structure each procedure by numbering the steps students must follow and requiring them to use them repeatedly in precisely the same order 3. To provide challenging activities that require the repetition of all basic processes to achieve automaticity 4. To breakdown any material to be taught to its smallest components and then organize them sequentially in planning 5. To provide all instructions or directions to students by telling, showing, and helping them to "walk, talk, or draw through" or otherwise rehearse these instructions to ensure their full understanding 6. To assume nothing and ask students to perform only those tasks for which they have the necessary tools and to start at the beginning and take ongoing inventory to check their knowledge in pertinent areas 7. To measure student progress in all areas throughout their training, not moving on to a new concept until 95 percent of the material is learned 8. To thoroughly teach the necessary arbitrary learning that cannot be discovered or inducted, such as the alphabet sequence and the basic sound-symbol relationships 9. To be flexible and creative in approaching each student and in persisting until every student has grasped and used the material 10. To plan daily lessons to ensure that students achieve near-perfect success and awareness

Pre- and Post-Testing	Use the Triple A Benchmark Assessment as a tool to continuously monitor reading/language progress to provide effective strategies as well as conduct periodic accountability reviews. This assessment measures a child's reading level based on where they are within one of the eight schedules. After each schedule, a student is given another assessment to determine if they are progressing, which identifies a child's strengths and weaknesses.
Trained Personnel	Trained CALTs, LDTs, and practitioners will work with students at their home or public or private school during the daytime.
Materials	Lessons are taken from eight schedules: I, IIA, IIB, IIC, IIIA, IIIB, IIIC, and IIID. Each schedule is dependent on knowledge taught in all preceding schedules. Therefore, all students, regardless of grade or reading level, should begin with Schedule I. By starting with Schedule I, a student can succeed daily in every language activity. To assist the group sessions, students will need the following additional materials. • Workbooks particular to each child's reading level • Plastic letters to reinforce both kinesthetic association of letter shapes and the visual identification of letters • An Initial Reading Deck, informally known as the Picture Deck • An Advanced Reading Deck, informally known as the Letter Deck • The Let's Read Series (Let's Read 4, Let's Read 5, and Let's Read 6) offers supplementary reading practice for selected schedule lessons • An alphabet strip that displays the alphabet in capital letters • A pencil frame that holds the pencil for the student, enabling their writing hand to remain in a relaxed position; designed to help students learn the appropriate pencil grasp and used in practicing both printed and cursive letters • The *Guideword Dictionary*, a practice book for developing skills in quickly locating entries in the dictionary
Monitoring	Students are continuously assessed, and their progress is constantly monitored.
Data Reporting	Teachers use a daily attendance sheet to track a student's attendance, which they use to help create a final progress report.

150

Program's Cost	**Materials:** Schedules: $100 per child **Intervention:** Miscellaneous items: $25 per child *Professional Development: Teacher training costs $5,000 for a two-year program, including observations and materials *Because this program occurs during regular work hours, teachers probably don't need to be paid an extra fee.
Program Duration	Students who lag two grade levels can learn read on their respective grade level once four schedules are completed in two and a half years. They can also advance to their respective grade levels ahead if all eight of the schedules are completed.
Curriculum **1.0 K–8 Decoding and Spelling Program**	Without early identification and intervention, reading difficulties typically persist into adulthood at least to the extent of hindering the enjoyment and productivity of reading. In some cases, it can affect job promotions and effective communication. The logic of all alphabetic languages, including English, is built on the understanding that every word is made up of a sequence of elementary speech sounds or phonemes, and these phonemes are represented by the letters. A failure of noticing phonemes and phonemic awareness in verbal memory skills, and often in their word retrieval abilities, is a major cause of profound reading disability for LD children. Such deficits are thought to result in the most common manifestation of poor reading, which is the difficulty in employing the alphabetic code to identify printed words. Our curriculum components include the following: • An explicit systematic decoding and spelling program for kindergarten through third grade • Emphasis on systematic decoding and encoding instruction and the study of word structure • Explicit and systematical skills, including multisensory instruction • A phonics and literacy program and training focused on systematically and explicitly taught skills and cumulative and scaffolding skills The Language Science Program for K–5 • An Alphabet Phonics (AP) Program • Decoding • The Take Flight Program (for 6–8) • The AP Benchmark • Decoding instrument (for K–3)

Intervention 2.0	Studies have shown that students with learning disabilities can lose up to 25 percent of their yearly academic gains over the course of the summer vacation. This is especially critical due to the lack of educational stimulation over the summer months at most homes. **The Summer Intervention Program** The Summer Intervention Program is designed for undiagnosed or diagnosed dyslexic and LD students who are performing below their respective grade levels in reading, writing, and math. The program's goal is to provide students with an academically enriching summer experience. Math and reading are targeted academic areas for improvement. Students who attend this program return to the fall semester better prepared to begin the school year. Summer Intervention Program Details: • One school • Four weeks in length • Held between June 5 to June 29 • Identified students from second to eight grades • Room for 50 students (7 per grade level with 1 extra spot that can be utilized anywhere) • 4 therapists with 12 students per therapist—students are split with multigrade levels Monday through Thursday sample daily schedule:

8:30 a.m.	Study skills in homeroom
9:00–10:00 a.m.	Reading
10:00–10:45 a.m.	Writing
10:45–11:00 a.m.	Break/snack
11:00–12:00 p.m.	Math
12:00 p.m.	Dismiss

Friday Field trips for all students are planned according to grade level grouping.

First-grade students begin with Schedule I and proceed sequentially through the eight schedules. Depending on an individual student's needs and the amount of time spent on the lessons each day, some will be able to complete most of the schedules in three school years. Students who need more intensive instruction at a slower pace will also benefit from the program's instruction.

Second- and third-grade students may be familiar with some of the beginning lessons from being in a regular classroom. Their reading level will be determined, based on the Triple A Benchmark. Once a child completes the program in three years, he/she will be reading at or above their respective grade levels.

The daily intervention program includes the following:

- Intervention for grades K–8
- Data collection to determine a student's placement into the given interventions
- Extensive practice that provides several opportunities for skills application
- The capability to monitor students throughout the program
- Extensive skill-based practice
- A fully operational progress-monitoring intervention system

Daily AP Program and Schedule Details

- Held Monday through Thursday
- 5 schools, with 30 students per school (total of 150 students)
- Utilizes a Language Science Program

Fridays are used for the following:

- An Administrative Day
- Reports/weekly summary writing
- Feedback
- Training
- As a Make-up day

Classroom Observations: Three given per year

Supportive Event: Parent Awareness Event

Reports

Daily Attendance Sheets

Attendance is checked daily and monitored throughout the program. Attendance is important in relation to the amount of success a child will have in the program. The more times he/she attends, the more they'll learn. To ensure success, a child needs to attend at least 150 out of the 185 sessions.

Monthly Graphemes Schedule

Each child's progress will be charted daily and weekly to determine where he/she is progressing in the schedule of lessons and activities.

Progress Reports:

- *Initial report*: Our trained professionals will provide a progress report that explains how the student's responses point to particular strengths and weaknesses involving the findings of the first assessment results.

- *Mid-term report*: This progress report, which is for the principal/parent, overviews the student's progress from the program's inception to where he/she is currently located in the individualized plan of services. It details the barriers the student may face in learning and enables instructor to make simple suggestions for classroom accommodations and lesson modifications and recommend activities for home and tips with schoolwork.

- *Final report:* At the end of the academic school year, this progress report is prepared to discuss the level of each child. It's given during the meeting between the principal and our trained professionals.

Staff Development 3.0	**TEACHER TRAINING PROGRAM** Research has proven that the key factor in learning to read is the difficulty linking letters with sounds. (Torgesen et al.,). The program's teachers will be trained to use a phonemic awareness screening instrument and the revised FOCUS Phonics Benchmark. Our teacher training program provides the content and depth of training necessary to enable teachers to provide appropriate instruction. In addition, it helps them make informed decisions about how to work with children and adults who suffer with learning differences or have reading disabilities. Once teachers complete this training, they have a conceptual foundation regarding reading acquisition and sources of reading difficulty. Other key aspects under our staff's development are as follows: • To provide training and coaching to teachers, instructional coaches, and administrators at various times throughout the year • To provide regular coaching visits complete with summary reports

- To provide onsite training for teachers, instructional coaches, school administrators, and district staff about the program focused on systematic phonics and the study of word structure

- To implement a fully operational progress monitoring system for teacher training

The Program's Structure

This training course is uniquely designed to teach classroom teachers, administrators, tutors, remedial reading specialists, curriculum supervisors, clinicians, speech language pathologists, and other professionals to implement a structured, sequential, multisensory curriculum for teaching language skills up to the level of literacy. It's an 80-hour introductory level course with 21 hours of additional workshop attendance required. Individuals can earn between 6 to 9 hours of graduate-level course credit from area universities.

Introductory course graduates who wish to receive certification as an Academic Language Therapist will gain in-depth knowledge of working with students with language learning differences in a two-year supervised program. These individuals must complete the advanced course, present demonstrations, and participate in curriculum workshops. All coursework must be completed within three years.

Completion of this two-year comprehensive training program prepares a teacher to receive a certificate of completion from Triple A Educational Services, Inc. with the title of Academic Language Therapist. Upon completion of a comprehensive examination by the Academic Language Therapy Association, our graduates will also receive the title of Certified Academic Language Therapist (CALT).

Curriculum

The curriculum is based on the Orton-Gillingham instructional theories and techniques. The core course requirements include conceptual foundations in the reading process; knowledge of the structure of language including phonetics, phonology, and morphology; and supervised practice in teaching reading. Other requirements include:

1. One week of initial training, and a final week of training, including a practicum component where each trainee has two one-hour tutoring sessions with a student who has experienced difficulty in reading

2. A total of 20-day practicum hours and 820 hours with children to be completed within the two-year program

3. Intensive instruction and supervision in learning phonetic and phonological language approach, as well as spelling, writing, and lesson planning

4. An apprenticeship program where the 20 teachers will serve under a Triple CALT for two years while working with students during in-school or after-school programs in group or private sessions

Supervised Teaching

Each teacher is required to implement and maintain remedial classes (with no more than 10 students per class) of academic language therapy with at least two groups/individuals in an appropriate setting each school day. Also, each teacher must prepare and submit periodic progress reports documenting their supervised teaching situations and clinical teaching hours.

Topics (determined annually)

Dyslexia 101

Executive Functioning Skills

ADHD

Number of Workshops:

Parents: Two workshops

Administrators: one workshop

Teachers: Two workshops

C. The TAME Action Plan

Goal	Time Line	Action Steps	Person(s) Responsible	Resources	Evidence of Success
Provide literacy interventions for struggling readers beginning in kindergarten		Analyze data about student needs, school capacity, and teacher knowledge Deciding on the methods and types of structured reading program to offer for these interventions	Principal, reading specialist	Test data Reading materials	Purchased materials
Purchase and implement a structured reading program to meet the students' needs	Summer school year	Identify students	District and school-testing coordinator	Test data	Student lists
		Research, identify, and purchase reading programs for targeted students	Principal, reading specialist	Information on reading programs, funds	Research notes, meeting agendas
		Identify an intensive reading course in the master schedule	Principal, assistant principal for the master schedule	A flexible master schedule	A finished master schedule
		Assign qualified teachers to the reading course	Principal, human resources (HR) personnel	Qualified teachers	A teacher list including their qualifications
		Place students in the course and monitor their progress	Principal, reading teachers	Course materials, professional development	Student grades, promotions, improvements on assessments

157

CPSIA information can be obtained
at www.ICGtesting.com
Printed in the USA
FSHW011127230419
57488FS

9 781457 566837